HIPPIE AT HEART SELF-HELP SERIES

FOLLOW THE TRAIL OF YOUR SPIRIT

A Fun, Sparky, Quasi-Shamanic, **Somewhat Serious Guide to Life Purpose**

MARGARET NASH

Printed in the United States of America.

ISBN: 978-1-0934371-5-7

Cover artwork by Marti McGinnis at HappyArt.com

Cover design: www. BookCoverMall.com

Book interior design: Dean Fetzer, GunBoss Books, www.gunboss.com

Contents

Download 'Meet Your Archetypes!'

A convenient, printable PDF version of the list of archetypes included in the book that you can work on when discovering your archetypes. Peruse, contemplate, make notes on it, sit with it under a tree.

Plus a bonus chapter chock full of more fun info on archetypes from ***Rebellious Aging: A Self-Help Guide for the Old Hippie-at Heart,*** also by Margaret Nash.

Each Archetype has a life lesson for you, a challenge and a purpose for being part of you. Understanding this purpose will help you discover your life purpose.

Learn how to interview your archetypes, recognize their Shadows, honor their contracts and hold Napoleon Hill type council meetings with them; among other useful and mind-expanding activities that will speed you toward your spirit trail.

Download your list and complimentary chapter here.

www.margaretnashcoach.com/free

Chapter 1

Follow the Trail of Your Spirit – the Search for Life Purpose

"You must follow the trail of your Spirit," he said.

I asked how such a trail could be known.

"It cannot be known by ordinary means.
Spirit trails are invisible.

You follow by intuition and observation.
The trail will be clear of obstacles.

When off the trail, many obstacles will be found.
When you meet resistance, you are off the trail.

Look for happenings, look for signs.
You must feel your way along, carefully watching,
watching, always watching."

Hopi Shaman – In the Valley of the Supreme Masters

There is something ephemeral about a trail. It's not exactly a path – rugged and clear – but instead delicate, ethereal and easy to miss if you don't know what you're looking for. Like the Shaman says, trails are not found by ordinary means, but they do leave clues, signposts.

This book can be your trail guide. Your guide to finding and following the trail of your life purpose.

You will know when you're on the trail because you will feel light, alive, motivated and energized. You will want to get out of bed in the mornings and there will be no resistance. (Well, maybe a little on cold mornings…) You will feel clear, aligned and focused on what *you know* is important to you. Life will be exciting.

And if you do fall off the trail and end up down some dead end in the forest, stuck and bewildered, this book will show you how to get back on track. It's all about following those signposts.

I'm a life-coach, so my approach to this subject is practical and results oriented. I'm going to take you through a structured process to discover a life purpose that will work for you at the stage of life you are in right here, right now. Every stage in life is different, so your requirements for a fulfilling, meaningful way to spend your time will be different from yesterday and maybe tomorrow.

We will together explore and identify your vision for your ideal lifestyle, what you're *really* good at, what your 'deep driving desires' are and what your archetypes are desperately trying to get you to do with your allotted span in this life time. They've been trying to get your attention for years and you and I are going to learn how to listen to them.

This book will be peppered with stories my clients encountered in their journeys along their spirit trails and how they found that sweet spot in work and life. It is my hope that these stories, plus my own long and winding tale of finding purpose will stimulate your thinking about how to start your own trail blazing experience.

It's the best trip you'll ever take.

The quest for purpose

I invite you to think about reading this book as standing at the trailhead of your *Hero's Journey* into the unknown landscape of your subconscious mind. Is that too new age-y for you? Maybe, but still, does it resonate a little or beckon to you?

Once you clearly identify your purpose it will seem so obvious you will wonder how you ever missed it. It will be staring you in the face.

At the very least it might get you off the sofa, away from the internet and politics; and as you forge ahead on your trail, you'll be, as Hunter S. Thompson would say, *"feeling fine, extremely sharp."*

(OK, so you don't have to look it up, it's in *Fear and Loathing in Las Vegas*.)

It's the journey that counts

You're going to love it, I promise. Not much fear and no loathing. It really is exciting and mind opening.

I repeat, your purpose today may be different from tomorrow. One day you may be writing a book, another painting a picture, another starting a business or a charity. Maybe you'll be hiking in the Himalayas or meditating in an ashram. You could be musing about life from your couch. Your purpose won't be a concrete commandment writ in stone. It's not static but moving, fluid, changing.

So don't book your ticket to Tibet just yet – your trail may lead you someplace different. Who knows, it may lead you on down here to Mexico. Mine did.

And you must never get complacent – staying true to your purpose requires *watching, watching, always watching,* using your intuition and remaining alert. You can fall off the trail for days, weeks, months, even years. But you can always find it again and bounce back. It's all here, in the following pages.

Please explain – what is the big deal about finding purpose?

I confess.

I've been obsessed with finding my life purpose – my burning desire and reason for living – for years now. It fascinates me. The implications are enormous. (Who says we even have a purpose? Who decides what it is? Is it predestined?)

After reading every book available on the subject and listening to countless webinars and seminars, my result was a huge amount of stress and frustration that simply increased the more I agonized over capturing this elusive unicorn. Life purpose needs to be something big, grand, or something that will leave a legacy. Right? I couldn't for the life of me think what would fit that bill.

Books and websites and trainers and self-help gurus proclaim the importance of finding your one unique life purpose. Without it, you are a lost soul, wandering in the desert; your life meaningless, frustrated and bereft of value.

I recently read about someone admitting to spending over $50,000 on one expensive life coach to discover her life purpose. And the answer she found? She was *meant to inspire.* Well shoot. I could have fed her that bromide for a lot less.

All I could think was: has finding life purpose become an indulgent first world pursuit bordering on self-obsession?

The psychologist Abraham Maslow would call it the quest for self-actualization, right at the top of his famous pyramid of needs. To recap his *Hierarchy of Needs*: Basic needs, security needs, social needs and at the top, self-actualization or self-realization. Once all the lower needs are satisfied, then we move up the hierarchy to the next stage, to higher callings, increasing our search for meaning and significance.

My grouch is simply this

Insisting people must find their life purpose in order to be complete – *the one unique, burning passion in life* – frequently causes unhappiness, not fulfillment. It's just overwhelming. Not to mention hard on the pocket.

Isn't the real desire lurking beneath the search for life purpose to find something to do with your time that feels productive, useful, meaningful and absorbing? And above all, that you enjoy?

So my proposal is this: chuck that great, big, overwhelming, baffling goal of finding *one grand life purpose* out the door and drop kick it to the curb. It's not serving you.

FOMO – The Feeling of Missing Out

The other day a client said to me, *"I feel such a sense that my life has no meaning, that it's all been a waste of time. And I feel intense jealousy or envy when I see colleagues who have made a success of things."*

I mused, *"Is it envy, or is it grief? Sadness over what you feel you've missed?"*

She started getting teary eyed at that point. *"Bingo. You got it. Grief."*

This client, by recognizing what was really happening to her, was able to let go and get on with creating a better life. What she thought was envy or resentment towards others was actually just sadness. And it was causing her to feel stuck.

Have you ever felt a sense of inexplicable sadness? The feeling you are missing out on something important but you can't quite put your finger on what it is?

This grief is a waste of energy. Regret, guilt. *If only I had...*

Being able to articulate a sense of purpose can free us from gloom and melancholy.

Many of my clients are retired and on the other side of 60 – but not all of them. And the younger ones are just as anxious to find meaning in what they do with their time.

I frequently hear the plea from the 60 plus group – *I haven't got all that much time left, so I want it to be well spent. Meaningful. I don't want to waste any more time doing things that I either don't enjoy or don't seem to make a difference.*

The younger clients are more interested in finding the right career. Purpose can be tied up with education, qualifications, niche, feeling at home somewhere. Semi-retired people can be just as concerned with finding satisfying things to do as they were when they were fully employed.

I've been there and maybe you have too. When that *what's my life purpose?* bee gets in your bonnet you can't easily get rid of it. I drove my friends and my own life coach crazy for years, agonizing over what my niche was, what I should focus on and my identity as a coach. My search included work issues. Yours may not. But the search for purpose is always activity related, i.e. *what should I be doing with my time?*

I'm here to tell you there are simple questions you can answer, a bit of soul searching, some experimenting, but you can drop any regret or guilt about how you've lived your life up until now. You can find your spirit trail, hop on it and enjoy your life, right here, right now. Just follow the chapters. There are lots of good, soul searching questions for you to play with.

What's it all about, Alfie?

The term *life purpose* is actually quite vague and there is no solid agreement about what it means, only allusions to intentions, direction, goals and plans. Let's get clearer on what we are talking about because each of us has a different interpretation. And that's fine. We don't have to agree. Just be clear what you are looking for.

- For many it will be how do I get my life to work? Who am I? What am I here for?
- For others it's a way to control time and create a legacy.
- Many are craving a *unifying thread* that links together the activities and experiences of their lives. A spiritual glue, or life theme, so to speak, that makes sense and holds it all together.
- For the vast majority it really boils down to, *how can I live a happy life?*

Supercoach author Michael Neill puts it this way:

"If your life had a message, what would that message be? What would you put on a billboard?"

The one agreed upon criteria is that when people are searching for life purpose it is for *something to do* that satisfies. Something that has value and makes one feel good about oneself.

Do you feel good about yourself, your life? If not, why not? Could it be you're off the trail and heading in the wrong direction?

Now, ask yourself:

Do I want a compelling obsession or simply nice things to do?

Nice things to do, or things to do that have significance?

How about all three? A compelling obsession that leads to nice things to do that have significance? Now that sounds intriguing.

The benefits of a sense of purpose

Feeling a sense of what you're here for can actually affect your life span. Studies show that those with purpose live longer and are happier than those who feel adrift *with no direction home*.

It is claimed that people who feel no sense of purpose are more prone to Alzheimer's disease than those with strong goals.

In interviewing earthquake and other disaster sufferers to find out why some survivors suffer PTSD (Post Traumatic Stress Disorder) and others don't, they found that by far the strongest factor was whether the person had a strong reason for living. It was associated with both lower PTSD and lower depressive symptoms. In almost every study having a purpose in life indicated a better emotional recovery from traumatic events.

Victor Strecher, in his book *Life Purpose* found that *"a strong, transcending purpose in life is good for your health and well-being and protects against disease and death."*

Shamans believe we get sick if we're not living our purpose. They call the chronic wasting autoimmune diseases such as fibromyalgia and chronic fatigue *Shaman sickness.* And their strong belief is that the cause and cure lie with the relationship to spirit.

Viktor Frankl, author of the iconic book, *Man's Search for Meaning*, based on his experiences in a Nazi death camp, observed that in the harsh and brutally terrifying camps, those inmates who spent their time serving others almost inevitably survived. In other words, those who had a purpose to live for and acted in alignment with their beliefs, were able to live a meaningful life in horrendous circumstances.

So searching for your purpose can be astonishingly satisfying. It's an important quest and worth the obsessing. It's my sincerest hope that it's worth your time to read this book and set off on your journey.

So I invite you to read on with me and together we will get you started on your trail.

Coaching question:

If your life had a message, what would that message be?

Chapter 2

Leap Like a Jaguar!

"When we reach the end of one of these lifetimes (other people would call them stages or phases in one's life), it's important to give the old self a decent burial and then leap like a jaguar into who we are becoming."
– Shaman, Healer, Sage.

I can remember as a little girl hearing about missionaries who went to the darkest depths of Africa to do their work. They believed they had been 'called by God' to spread his gospel and they obeyed without question. I recall feeling full of dread that God might call *me* to go work somewhere on the other side of the planet, away from family and friends in strange and terrifying territory and I would have no choice but to surrender. It did not appeal.

Now (leaving aside whether you approve of mission work or not), today I imagine those missionaries probably loved every moment and deepest, darkest Africa was sunny and bright. They may have felt God chose them, but they also chose to go. But I didn't see that then. I prayed mission work wasn't my calling.

Swami SarvaPriyananda, Hindu monk and YouTube rockstar, (check him out) of the Vedanta Society of New York says that his happiest time was when he was in his apprenticeship to become a monk and had to live completely on his own in the Himalayas, with no possessions and begging for his food. He said an intense feeling of liberation and peace pervaded his being and he was without worries or anxiety. But his purpose lay elsewhere so he eventually came down off the mountain.

Who knew? Things are not always what they seem. But I imagine for most of us these wouldn't be our first choices for life purpose.

Here are a few beliefs I hold about finding purpose.

We don't have one purpose that we have to find – we *choose* from a myriad of possibilities.

There is a big difference between believing there is one great all encompassing mission that you have been born to fulfill (and that may send you to Africa or the Himalayas) and the idea that there are a whole slew of things you can choose from. To me it's obvious that we can choose.

> *"There are a great number of possible futures and possible outcomes for every person. Our beliefs transform some of those possibilities into probabilities..." – MG Hawkins*

Read that last sentence again. "Our beliefs transform some of those possibilities into probabilities."

So what we think and feel and believe about opportunities in life, have an effect on which ones will work for us.

In other words,

We have a say in how we want to live our lives.

We can choose.

It's up to us to create the life we want with our preferences, choices and lifestyle. We can't blame anyone else if we don't at least make an effort. All we can do is try.

Unfortunately, too much choice causes stress. Making decisions is difficult. The more we have to choose from, the more difficult the decision-making. It's the Starbucks Syndrome – too many different types of coffee to choose from, so you give up and go home instead.

This may sound counter-intuitive, but this book is going to help you *limit* your choices in order to make it easier for you. Latte or Americano? That's it.

There are a number of trails you can jump on and none of them is necessarily wrong. You've got to try it out and see if it's working for you. I want to help you find the one that really makes your heart sing.

A life purpose needs to include creative, compelling self-expression.

In order to be authentic, our purpose must express who we are. Therefore your true authentic purpose cannot be chosen for you by some nebulous spiritual being, nor by your parents and society.

For it to be *your* compelling self-expression you need to have a say in forming it. For that you need to dig deep to understand who you are.

Henry David Thoreau famously said,

"One is not born into the world to do everything but to do something."

So, what is your 'something'?

Ask: What am I willing to change, sacrifice, or give up, in order to find my something? Would I go to the symbolic Africa? Climb that mountain and live in a cave?

What drives your search?

In Vedanta, the study of the ancient Indian Vedas, one of the teachings is that when we desire something, it's always a desire for freedom *from* something. In other words, we don't desire security, we desire freedom from insecurity. We don't desire power, we desire freedom from feeling weak and vulnerable; we don't want pleasure so much as we want freedom from suffering and boredom.

What frequently drives the search for purpose is fear and pain: fear of never arising above the mediocre, of never achieving anything of significance and pain from the desperate notion that I will never accomplish what I was meant to do in life.

Most of us don't want to face the question, *was it all a waste of time?*

Deepak Chopra, the well-known author and teacher, says

"It's not dying we fear, but the fear of not having fully lived."

Have you ever felt any of these fears?

- Not fulfilling your potential.
- Feeling useless or irrelevant.
- Getting older – what will it bring?
- Wasting time.
- Being bored.
- Missing out.
- Feeling disconnected.

Martha Beck, Life-Coach, says her clients searching for purpose exhibit *"a querying, relentless, urgent need to connect with their true nature."*

The Philosopher's Stone

The Philosopher's Stone is a legendary alchemical substance capable of turning base metal into gold or silver. It is also called the elixir of life, useful for rejuvenation and for achieving immortality. I'm going to show you how to use this medieval metaphor in creating your purpose.

We create our life purpose out of the ingredients of our life experiences and choices.

Every teeny tiny experience, good and bad, you have had in life can be used in forming your purpose. Nothing you have done, learned, or experienced needs to be wasted.

Here is where the alchemy comes in: finding your niche in life means building on what you've learned, suffered, and the mistakes you have made and transmuting it into activities that serve you and help others.

The ultimate alchemy is channeling your pain into art, writing, mentoring, starting a business, healing, teaching, or being a nicer person. Mistakes, accidents and bad life choices become tools for growth.

Derek Doepker, coach and best selling writer says

"I've found when I made my failures not just about my own growth, but about failing in order to help others avoid the mistakes I made, I was able to overcome many of my fears."

He calls this his 'Case Study Mindset',' which he named when he realized his greatest breakthroughs came when he took whatever challenges he was facing as an experiment, game, or case study.

The Wounded Healer

The best healers are those who have overcome illness and tragedy. So if you have been sick or damaged in some way, you can heal, learn and evolve from it to help others.

Joe Dispenza, scientist, lecturer and author, started his healing mission after he overcame paralysis from a horrible accident in his early 20s. He refused orthodox treatment that could have left him in a wheelchair for the rest of his life and remarkably healed himself through various alternative methods. His story is quite inspiring. He transmuted his tragedy into triumph and has had an incredibly successful career helping others overcome illness.

Think of it this way. The people who are top of their professions, the most successful in life, are those who have made lots of mistakes, overcome hardships and challenges and transmuted them into ways to serve others.

- The best coaches are those who have overcome issues and challenges.
- The best person to help you quit smoking is someone who used to smoke.
- The best person to help you in business is someone who has failed, picked him or herself up again and gone on to succeed.
- The best person to help you lose weight is someone who was overweight and has lost that weight.
- The best shaman is the one who has survived an ordeal by fire.
- A lot of really great artists – musicians, painters, sculptors, writers – create their best work from pain.

You are no different. Your mistakes and failures are your goldmine. And we're going mining.

Time to leap?

At the beginning of this chapter I quoted Alberto Villoldo, a medical anthropologist in his book *Shaman, Healer, Sage*.

Here is the quote again,

> *"When we reach the end of one of these lifetimes (other people would call them stages or phases in one's life), it's important to give the old self a decent burial and then* ***leap like a jaguar into who we are becoming****."*

Maybe it's time for you to *leap like a jaguar* onto your Spirit Trail. Are you ready?

This book is an invitation to come on this magical mystery gold mining tour of your spirit. The rest of the book will point out and describe signposts to look for that will help you identify your best activities, doing what you love, sticking to the trail and not wandering off into the forest. It will be practical and useful, as well as a teeny bit mystical.

All set? Now…LEAP!

Coaching question:

What are you willing to sacrifice in order to find and live your purpose?

Chapter 3

Create Your Vision

"You must view life as an adventure, and opposition and difficulties as challenges within that adventure. It is your adventure – it belongs to you along with the freedom to create whatever you desire." – MG Hawkins

You leapt. Like a jaguar.

You must have or you wouldn't be reading this far. You leapt onto *the Trail of Your Spirit* into who you are becoming. Now it's time to become acquainted with the first signpost you will encounter on the trail to make sure you are headed in the right direction.

The first signpost on the quest to find life purpose is to **get really clear about what you want** and **create your vision** for what your purpose needs to look like.

Clarify your intentions. Create your vision. Remember, if *you* are not clear about your vision, nature abhors a vacuum and will fill it with someone else's vision – something you may not want. Have you noticed that when things turn out in a way you're not happy with, you probably weren't really certain what you did want instead? Once we get clear, things tend to fall into place more easily.

One thing is certain – we all want different things and we all have different ideas about what our purpose should look like. Isn't the real desire lurking beneath the search for life purpose to find something to do with your time that feels productive, useful, meaningful and absorbing? And above all, that you enjoy?

Some of us are looking for an *activity* and others for *a way of being* or expressing ourselves. A good vision will include both. Let's create it.

So we will go ahead and put some ingredients in the pot, cook it up, stir it and see what comes out. The best cooks are creative and don't follow recipes. They make up their own.

Here are some of the ingredients we will need:

Question: Do you really want a compelling obsession or fun and interesting things to do?

No judgment here, this is just for you. I know many retired people who simply want something to do that seems useful and enjoyable and doesn't feel like a waste of time. The truth is they enjoy their lives and don't want a big upheaval. They just feel something is lacking. Others may want to be totally obsessed with a cause, or art, or service of some kind.

Answer the question and throw that in to start simmering.

Question: What are you willing to sacrifice to find and fulfill your purpose?

Be honest with yourself. You may not be willing to sacrifice anything, or give up very much for your purpose, so that is an ingredient you must put into the pot. Or you may be just about willing to give up a few hours of internet or Netflix to get it going. It's up to you...and you. Just don't lie to yourself. This may need a stir-fry to make it palatable.

(This one is very challenging for me. I'm an internet addict and spend much too much time on the computer or watching Netflix. I know I have to sacrifice some of this time wasting if I really want to be productive and spend my time well.)

But you may be willing to move continents for your burning desire.

Question: What are your constraints?

They are usually around money, time, age, health and family duties. Ignore at your peril.

Money: Do you need to make money? That can be a huge constraint on your vision. Survival comes first. You may not be able to open your hand-made oriental kite shop just yet if you need to put food on the table. It won't make money for a while. Not yet. Sling that in the pot. Don't leave it out – it's a crucial ingredient.

Time: How much time do you have to devote to this? Is family a factor in what you do? Do you have to fit your writing in at 5am before work? Do you babysit or have children to look after? Or are you retired and have all the time in the world...that you are currently devoting to Facebook? We're all friends here.

Health: How's your energy? If you are older and have a few health issues, you may not be able to take off to deepest Africa to help orphan elephants. If you are high maintenance then a tent in the Sahara while you study the desert hedgehog and his habits might not be practical.

My retired-Presbyterian-preacher father flew off to Nepal to run an international church in Katmandu in 1980 immediately after retirement; he dropped dead six months into his stint from heart failure. He was following his dream, but not taking his health or general fitness into account. Katmandu is very high altitude.

You'd be ill advised to ignore health. Your recipe could poison you without it.

(My constraints are mainly around energy. As such, I'm not willing to work full time anymore. I have no family responsibilities and my time is my own. I like lots of couch time with the dogs. Who's noticing?)

What are your criteria? Details, measures, benchmarks, specifics

We've got some of the basics, now what is going to add flavor? What are your *criteria*?

Let me help you here. I'll give you mine. My purpose needs to be:

- Work related (it's what challenges me)
- Money making (it's what validates what I'm doing)
- Learning something new (keeps me interested)
- Fun
- Feeling organized, in control
- Feeling like I'm good at something (not immediately recognizable!)
- Not time wasting (My Calvinist Presbyterian upbringing)
- Feeling comfortable in my own skin – congruent, authentic
- Making use of my skills, talents and experience
- Feeling good about the way I'm living.

- Feeling like I'm living a good life, a fulfilled life and helping others to as well.
- Advancing spiritually, emotionally, physically
- Related to personal evolution.

Not much to ask, huh?

Now, what are *your* criteria for your life purpose? Work related? Service oriented? Full time? Part time? Now and then? Fun? Meaningful? All of the above?

Something that keeps you on the straight and narrow? I know a retired sound engineer who has set up a studio in his house and does a bit of recording for people when he feels like it. *Keeps me out of trouble*, he says. His wife agrees.

Some people are helpers and thrive within the structure of charity work or church work, working within a group. Is this you? If so then you may want to start looking at the different organizations in your community.

Others prefer just opening themselves up to whatever opportunities come their way during the day. Maybe that resonates. If so you may want to focus on setting that as a goal every day and making it a habit to look for chances to serve and learn and connect.

Some like to ask themselves before each day begins – what's on offer for me today? What am I meant to learn, whom am I meant to meet?

"Flow into every nook and cranny, every possibility that opens in your life. You'll be young for a hundred years."
– Martha Beck

A growing number of folks these days don't want to retire completely and prefer to pursue semi-retirement. (Hands up, that's me.)

Others like doing business and want to make money.

I don't need to work for a living, but I like the independence of making my own money. It somehow validates what I do. As a female it gives me a sense of being able to look after myself. Without making money, what I do seems like a hobby and for some reason I balk at that. The word *hobby* sounds like a time filler to me. I don't want to fill my time; I want to use it.

Choose ingredients for your recipe. Create it.

Remember if you don't have your very own vision, others will impose theirs on you. Nature abhors a vacuum, all that.

Here's a shortcut to all of the above if you are impatient. I call it my ***Let's Get Real Strategy.***

I would love to find my life purpose.

- I am not willing to… (move, change jobs, go to Africa, etc)
- I am willing to… (change careers, work full time, go on a course)
- I might be willing to… (get up earlier, change my schedule, limit time on the internet)

A day well spent…

The other day I was fooling around on YouTube, wasting time (!), looking for anything to entertain and distract me from doing something more challenging. I frequently find subjects, sometimes bizarre, that hold my interest for a period of time before I move on to something new.

At this point I was intrigued by a plethora of videos on van life. All about people of no fixed abode who live in vans – mobile homes, RVs (recreational vehicles), motorhomes, campervans, even converted school buses. Minimalist, nomadic, traveling and on the move all the time, sleeping in national parks, Wal-Mart parking lots, or simply parked on residential streets.

Don't get me wrong; it does not appeal to me at all, I'm much too high maintenance, but I'm fascinated by the idea of living that way, so very different from my own comfortable lifestyle.

Van lifers have communities, tribes. They keep in touch with each other, make videos for YouTube and prearrange meet ups in designated areas. They are always on the move. Many work online and spend a lot of time in Starbucks making money from their computers.

Van lifers take great pride in their few belongings, are for the most part well organized, clean and Spartan. They value independence and a sense of freedom. They are their own bosses and no one dictates how they spend their time.

But it's hard! And you have to be constantly cleaning, tidying, looking for places to stop and camp for the night, vigilant about potential dangers most of us don't even consider. Pros and cons, in other words.

"Freedom's just another word for nothing else to lose..."

This particular day I came across a video made by a young man in the US, in his 30s, who had sold up everything and taken to the road with his small home. He loved it.

And his story about why he had chosen this life was interesting. (I would love to share the link, but I'm sorry I lost it.)

This is his story. Years before, his father, whom he loved deeply, had been planning to get out on the road and live life free and independently. He had spent his entire working life at a job that earned his keep and fed the family but wasn't his joy or passion. He longed to retire, hit the road and really *start living his life*. It was his time: he could leave work with a pension, his wife had died years earlier so he had no one to answer to and the kids were grown and settled.

He sold his home, bought his dream RV and set out in the direction of Yosemite. The mountains! Nature! Freedom!

A few months into his journey he dropped dead of a heart attack. Gone. His stunned and grieving son decided to live the life his father had missed. He didn't want to wait until he was 65 to start living his dream. What was he waiting for?

So he took the little RV and made it his home.

At first he found it hard and missed the stability of normal life, but after a while began to embrace his *Inner Gypsy* and settled in to his new transient lifestyle. He began to love it passionately. He made friends, wonderful friends. He set up a successful online business. He was his own boss. His parting words on the video really struck me; he said that what really made it all worthwhile was that at the end of the day, despite it being tough and challenging, what he loved was he could look back and feel it was *a day well spent.*

Wow. *A day well spent.* Aren't we all looking for this? Days well spent turn into weeks and months and years and finally, a life well spent.

It seems like the search for purpose and meaning really boils down to this – wanting to feel your time is well spent. And while it was striking to see in a young man, it usually becomes more important as we get older, retire, kids leave home and we begin to be aware that our time on this planet is limited. We simply want to feel we are spending it well.

Do you feel you are spending your time well? Is what you are doing satisfying, fulfilling a purpose, meaningful, interesting and challenging?

If not, what are you waiting for?

A day well spent was the prime ingredient of this young man's recipe. The secret sauce.

So your Vision is the first signpost to the trail of your spirit. Spend some time pulling it together. Answer the questions and list your criteria. Figure out your constraints. This will move you in the right direction on your trail.

MG Hawkins in his book on Tibetan shamanism relates a message from one of the shamans about setting goals and having visions. It's worth sharing.

"Maintain the image (of the goal) but do not struggle to keep it exactly as you began. Let the image play, let it come alive. Maintain it but let it live. Watch very carefully the image. It will take on life, it will change...
Your desire is to receive the expanded image, not create it."

Your vision is dynamic, not static. Let it breathe, let it live. Treat it like you would a spark when starting a fire; carefully blow into it and let it come to life. Then enjoy the fire you have helped to start.

So let the vision dance for you – don't force it because then it will come from your intellect and not from your spirit.

Your task

Start the process of creating a vision of what you want your life purpose to look like. Take a notebook and write out what you want from your life purpose and why you are looking for it. It can be in any form that works for you – stream of consciousness, a bullet list, or a paragraph. Include what you want to avoid and what you want freedom from, by finding it – in other words, the downside of not bothering to look for it.

1. **Do you want a compelling obsession or simply fun and interesting things to do?** Or both? Remember, a compelling obsession might mean you end up in Katmandu looking after elephants and require a lot of energy. Are you up for that?
2. **What are you willing to sacrifice to find and fulfill your purpose?** Time on the couch? Less Facebook? Giving up a successful money making job? Be honest – nobody's looking.
3. What are your constraints around money, time, age, health and family duties? This is not the same as obstacles – it's about being realistic.
4. **What are your criteria?** Work related? Service oriented? Full time? Part time? Now and then? Fun? Meaningful? Social? Constraints be damned, I'm shooting for the moon? Check out my personal list above to get you started.

You've started creating your vision. It's not set in stone and any of it can change and morph. Kindle it and get the fire blazing.

Now, on to the next signpost on the trail. This one is oh, so practical and not at all woo-woo. Keep your notebook handy.

Coaching question:

If you could wave a magic wand and be able to do anything that you wanted to do with your life, what would that look like?

Chapter 4

Which Comes First: Passion or Skill?

"Were it not for the leaping and twinkling of the soul, man would rot away in his greatest passion, idleness."
– Carl Jung

Some would say the next signpost on the trail of your spirit should be about passion and desire, but I beg to differ. Bear with me. Is the advice to follow your passion the secret to happiness or the worst advice ever? Untangle this ball of yarn with me.

Some people are born with their purpose in life marked out for them. They know at an early age that they want to be concert pianists, or artists, or missionaries. My Presbyterian preacher father grew up on a farm in rural Virginia in the early part of the twentieth century. From as far back as he could remember he knew he wanted to be a preacher. It was his calling.

Mozart was playing the piano at age five; Rafael Nadal picked up a tennis racket at age three.

Tiger Woods was born with a golf club in his hand (I could swear that's not fake news). Shirley Temple, singing and dancing.

Lucky them. Most of us haven't got a clue. We weren't born with an overwhelming passion or purpose that defines our identity and we don't know what we are here to do. We have to figure that out as we go along.

Malcolm Gladwell, writer for *The New Yorker*, author of five best sellers (*Tipping Point, Blink, Outliers*, among others) and social science maven says, *"You should pursue what interests you, not what you're good at.*" He goes on to say that passion gets you further than some *dry notion of ability*. Wham!

Steve Jobs, founder of Apple Computers, is famously quoted as saying, "*You've got to find what you love...if you haven't found it yet, keep looking, don't settle."*

What these highly successful people are saying, summed up in a succinct sound byte, is *follow your passion* – a popular mantra for many searching for purpose and success in life.

Hard to argue with Steve Jobs

But is it good counsel? Hard to disagree with on the surface – it sounds exciting, motivating and oh so modern. Problem is, Jobs didn't follow his own advice. He didn't start out passionate about designing computers and he wasn't really all that tech smart. He wasn't even interested in starting a business. He was passionate about Zen meditation. Apple Computers kind of evolved – into the most successful company in the world.

Follow your passion may seem hard to argue with, but Cal Newport does just that. Newport is another best selling author of five books on career success, as well as a professor of Computer Science at Georgetown University. Not someone to be sneezed at.

He says *follow your passion* is bad advice. Full stop.

Newport claims most of us don't have a pre-existing passion that's useful or has career potential. Popular passions may be football, or baking, or photography, or swimming, but these are interests that frequently don't translate into successful careers. He quotes numerous real life examples of people failing at attempts to make a career out of their passions.

Not to mention coming up short as a life purpose.

Rare and valuable skills are what we need

According to Newport, following a passion is a depressingly bad strategy for success in life. He says a better strategy instead is to build up competence and look for *rare and valuable skills* we can develop and just simply get good at something.

From there passion develops, not the other way around. As you get better at something, your passion for it grows.

Newport recommends what he calls 'deep work': an intense focus and concentrated *nose to the grindstone* effort on one skill for a period of time until you build up expertise. Work with no interruptions, no social media, no breaks, until you master something that was difficult for you and had interest for you. Not necessarily passion.

I think this is relevant at whatever stage of life you are. I'm semi-retired and have found Newport's ideas intensely motivating – helping me to focus on what I really want to do by looking at what I'm already good at. At my age I'm not feeling inclined to spend time on something where I don't already have some sort of skill or affinity.

Have you noticed how few people grow up wanting to be realtors, or hedge fund managers, or business consultants? I never envisioned being a life coach, nor did I dream of personal development training. Yet people frequently fall into similar satisfying and lucrative careers by developing skills rather than intent.

What about you? Do you think it's better to pursue your passion, or develop your skills and watch your passion develop?

Or...both?

Cal Newport is right on so many points he makes. Do you know someone who has followed his or her passion only to fail miserably?

What could go wrong following passion?

I recently heard about a fellow here in San Miguel who had been hit hard by an unfortunate experience.

His story: he was an excellent cook and had some killer recipes that had proven popular where he had been living. So he decided to up stakes and sink all his savings into a seaside café in a popular beach resort on the coast of Mexico, near Cancun.

What could go wrong? He had experience cooking for a restaurant and must have felt he knew enough about that world to make a success on his own. He had money to get started. Apparently what he didn't have was the necessary savvy to run a business in a foreign country in a highly competitive tourist area. It can be vicious.

Someone, probably a competitor, vandalized his café before it got started; he didn't have insurance, end of story. He's now back in San Miguel feeling a bit bewildered and with wallet and confidence severely impacted.

How often does this happen? People who are excellent cooks decide to start a restaurant only to lose their life savings because they haven't got an ounce of business acumen or street smarts? The stories are legion.

Or someone sets up a dog rescue only to end up with too many dogs and no way to pay for their care, because they didn't have sufficient finance or a place to look after them properly before they began picking up pups off the street?

Or someone in England who loves nothing more than an evening in the pub drinking a pint or two with his friends and has always fancied the idea of owning his own pub, finally sinks all his money into his dream and then finds he's bored to tears serving drinks every night? He loved drinking, not serving.

The list is endless. *Blindly* pursuing a passion can end in disaster.

Cat rescue calamity

Another lady I met set up a cat rescue center here in Mexico. She adored cats and her heart broke in a million pieces whenever she encountered a homeless feline. Convinced her calling in life lay with cat caring, she set up a rescue center in her home. She loved cats, after all and she couldn't imagine having too many.

Soon she could. With no funding arranged, she quickly ran out of money for food and vet bills. Cat litter was expensive. Cats need to be sterilized early on or you will soon end up with many more than you bargained for. She called on all the people who said they would love to help – before – and watched as they melted into the Mexican campo. Her home slowly degenerated into ruin as fur and arresting aromas took over. Every room was fully occupied with four-legged lodgers.

I never knew what became of all the cats. It was hard to get them rehomed because no one wanted to come inside and meet them. Plus she indulged in a few complaining posts on Facebook threatening to have all the cats put to sleep if no one stepped forward to help – she didn't mean it but scarce donations quickly dried up.

Anyway, you get my point. A little business and marketing acumen was needed. Funds acquired and a helper hired. Cages built. Some research in looking after animals would have helped. Liaising with a local vet. A little planning would have gone a long way plus a little expertise in something other than kitty cuddling. They don't call it blind passion for nothing.

10,000 hours. Really?

Malcolm Gladwell, in his book, *Outliers*, famously quotes research indicating we need to spend 10,000 hours to gain expertise in any given area. To put it in perspective, that's a full time job for five years.

He uses the Beatles as an example – everyone assumed back in 1964 when the Fab Four burst upon the music scene, that the lads from Liverpool were an overnight success. In fact, despite being quite young, they had put in their 10,000 hours of effort perfecting their craft by working for several years in a nightclub in Hamburg, Germany. There they worked eight hours a day, six days a week, in a seedy bar and hammered away at singing and playing. By the time they hit the international scene they were seasoned performers, able to handle the limelight. They had earned it.

Outliers was a huge success and the 10,000-hour rule was quoted everywhere. Martha Beck, well-known international life coach, uses it extensively in her book, *How to Find Your Way in a Wild New World.* When discussing life purpose she asks you to identify what it is you have spent 10,000 hours on in your life and to focus on that because that is where your skill and expertise will lie.

My problem with this and I think I may not be alone, is that many of us can't think of anything on which we have spent so much time, except maybe television or reading.

Ack. This doesn't inspire or help much. I once joined a Tai Chi class only to quit in despair after the teacher repeatedly told us it would take at least twenty years to get to any level of competence. Ditto for an art class where the very talented teacher told us it had taken her forty years to be able to paint the way she did.

Now if I had been in my twenties, this might have spurred me on to excellence, like the 17-year-old George Harrison in Hamburg. But I was in my fifties and just kept thinking, *I haven't got time for this*. Shame I quit: had I stuck with either I might be pretty good by now.

But let's look at this research on the 10,000-hour rule more closely, which came originally from the work of K. Anders Ericsson at the University of Florida. Ericsson studied professional athletes, world-class musicians, chess grand champions, Olympians and other ultra competitors who were at the top of their game. He worked out from interviews that most had put in 10,000 hours of intense effort to get to *the top of the heap.*

In popular culture, this idea morphed from being a requisite for world-class expertise – to being really good at something – to a requirement for simply learning something new.

And now the commonly held belief is that we need 10,000 hours of practice to learn anything new! I bet you've heard it quoted. It's wrong. We don't. You need 10,000 hours to get to *world-class level* at something. Like an Olympic gymnast. Like the Beatles.

Josh Kaufman, (TedTalk) says we actually only need *20 hours* of intense deep effort to get reasonably good at a new skill. So forty-five minutes a day of focused, deliberate practice for about a month should produce basic skill in just about any area.

Better! I like that! That means I can pursue a passion, even at a late date in life, with a reasonable chance of getting pretty good at it. This works for me!

But do we need both skill and passion?

There is no question that without passion or intense interest you are hardly likely to find joy in your work. When times are tough, you will feel inclined to quit. So yes, we do need to love what we do. That's what will get us out of bed in the morning, bright-eyed and bushy-tailed and ready to work. That's what will give meaning to our lives and keep us young (or at least bushy-tailed).

I think when we talk about finding life purpose most of us have a vision of doing something we love, that is compelling, that we can lose ourselves in.

Compelling self-expression. Compelling *creative* self-expression. This is where the trail lies. Because you need a compelling passion, but to put that compelling passion to good use, you also need to combine it with skill.

So I'm going to take you through some practical steps to find your *practical compelling creative self-expression* – the activity that fits those descriptions and will make both Cal and Malcolm happy.

Let's start with skills and competence and figure out what you can do. Come on, you know there's *something*!

Coaching question:

What is easy for you that others find challenging?

Chapter 5

What Can You Already Do Well?

"What one skill, if you developed and did it in an excellent fashion, would have the greatest positive impact on your life? This should become the focal point for personal development." – Brian Tracy

Skills, talents, abilities, things you are trained in and areas of expertise, are crucially important in formulating your purpose. They bear first consideration, sweeping aside your secret desires and unfulfilled passions. That sounds counter-intuitive, but we discussed why this is such an important distinction in the previous chapter.

Passion without skill can lead to disaster, failure and frustration. Not to mention bankruptcy.

Unbridled passion needs the bridle of competence.

This is a working chapter. Notebooks out please. We are going to identify your skills and proficiencies – all of them, not just the rare and valuable ones. You've got a lot more than you think.

Answer these questions as best you can. We want to record a time line, a storyline all about you.

What are you good at?
Write down everything from cooking to trigonometry to growing tomatoes. Can you drive? Put it down. One good recipe will do.

What qualifications, certificates and degrees have you earned along the way?
Include that weekend Reiki certificate, the course in ceramics, the week in Santé Fe playing with past life regression. Even that course in dog training and that commercial driving license which means you can drive trucks on ice roads in the arctic.

If you could give advice to your younger self about directions to take in life, what would it be? What would you want to learn that you didn't? What line of work would you take if you had it to do over?
Learn Spanish, learn Spanish, learn Spanish. You never know where you're going to end up living.

What rare and valuable skills do you have?
What do you find easy that others find difficult? That means anything that not *everybody* can do easily, so binge watching Netflix (which a lot of us are very good at) doesn't count. It may be something you take for granted because it's so natural for you, but not for others.

I can talk in front of large groups and love it. I was surprised to learn that my enjoyment is not universal; on the contrary, it's frequently listed as one of life's greatest fears. So I count public speaking as one of my valuable skills.

What resources would you need to get really *excellent* at something in which you are already skilled?
Another course in Santa Fe? 20 hours of deep work? A coach? A new computer? A place to write or paint?

Now, with these questions and answers in mind, I'm going to ask you to write *your* story, based on your experience, education, skill sets. But first I will tell you my story, so hang in there, don't snooze. Hearing the journey someone else took can sometimes help you clarify your own life story.

I come from Alabama...

I grew up in Alabama, the Deep South, without any discernable skills that I can recall, but great enthusiasm for boys and dating, cats, makeup, the Beatles and reading. Not much to work with there. Can you relate?

I seemed to have zero affinity for math or science of any genre and my teachers pretty much agreed on this. I was quite typical of southern girls of my generation. (Feminists, bristle here. It gets worse.)

I was good at English, the reading bit, and loved philosophy, psychology and political science, but not enough to buckle down and get serious. No deep study.

Psyche 101 was as far as I got with psychology because I couldn't do statistics.

My extracurricular activities during my high school years were sitting on the phone for hours (Do you remember doing that? Phones that hung on the wall and had long cords you had to pull around a corner to get some privacy?), dating on the weekends (heaven forbid you didn't have a date!), driving around in the car, going to church and hanging out at McDonalds (It was a new thing then, cool, like internet cafes when they first opened).

Nothing much else comes to mind. I'm sure I did an art class and I seem to remember piano lessons, but the rest is a blank.

I was a good student and reasonably smart, but I wasn't really outstanding at anything. Don't cry, I had a pretty good time.

Off at college I majored in Religion and Philosophy. I was enthusiastic and nerdy about the theme, but it wasn't exactly practical. I think it was probably one of the only subjects I was guaranteed not to fail, so it was a default major. Nobody failed Religion: the department had too few people signing up and those that did were treated like royalty. I also liked that it kind of confused people. I didn't strike anyone as the pious or intellectual type. In my funny way it was rebellious.

Once again, no real deep study, just enough to be able to yak in an intelligent sounding way about subjects nobody else knew much about.

Hey, I was pretty good at erudite sounding conversation. And very good at convincing people that I knew what I was talking about. Hang onto that thought. I later became a sales and business trainer and those are pretty useful skills to have in that arena.

I fancied myself a lawyer…but law school? Bar exams? Forget it. I got married right out of college so a law career was not going to happen. (Hey, we did the marriage thing early back in those days. More bristling.)

After college graduation, followed quickly by marriage, I cast about for something to do and the usual threesome of career possibilities for educated Southern ladies came to mind: social worker, teacher, librarian. I'm not kidding, that was it for career advice back then, back there.

So I trundled off to Library College in London to learn how to shelve books and be a librarian. *Information Science* they called it and I'm hoping it hasn't been kicked to the curb by the computer.

Let me just say here, this was not a passionate career choice. It was more, well, I like books and I like to read and I would like some sort of job qualification so what the heck? A post-grad year of library college in central London was quite fun. Shame about the job.

Could there be a less suitable career for me?

I don't think so. I was living in England and a loud mouthed, blonde, rather over- confident American among the quiet British bookshelves was interesting for all concerned. Except me. I nearly went crazy.

So I bumbled my way into real estate and things started to pick up a bit. I seem to recall I just marched down to the High Street of my English town, walked in the first Estate Agency (that's British for realtor) and asked for a job. To his credit the first realtor I spoke to offered me a job on the spot, starting then and there. I didn't even go home. He saw some potential.

Now this was fun. I found I really was very good at selling and for once I was developing *a useful skill.* I also discovered a competitive streak in me that I had to rein in at times. But here my loud mouth American accent and direct manner stood me in good stead.

My colleagues thought Americans knew all there was to know about selling, so watched me with concealed, slightly disapproving, but very close attention. Americans did seem to be better at selling, at least back then. I found it quite easy to bulldoze my way to the top of the heap.

Then a strange thing happened. After a few years and a lot of success, I began to realize a hotshot realtor wasn't *who I am.*

Something wasn't fun any more. I felt inauthentic. I no longer relished being hated and reviled by jealous wannabes. So I quit…

…and went into sales training. This provided a new buzz. *I was able to use my experience in selling and put it to good use* without having to do the selling. It was challenging and exciting. I was also able to hone my natural affinity for public speaking.

This was better than actual selling. I decided to branch out.

I extended my sales training into business and management training. (Remember my skills at sounding like I knew stuff? Handy here.) I developed a successful career as a consultant and trainer, *building on what I already knew and had natural skills in, plus my experience.* Keep this point in mind.

In the mid 90s I kept getting requests from my clients for training in something called NLP (Neuro-linguistic Programming). So I went on a weekend seminar to learn all about it. I emerged giddy, drooling and spaced out, four years later – after spending thousands of pounds and a big chunk of time indulging my obsessive interest – a certified expert in NLP and Hypnosis.

Here was the genesis of a *passion* for personal development

I adored all the new ideas in psychology and self-help along with cutting–edge pragmatic approaches to training and coaching. I felt I had finally hit my stride, found my niche, discovered my calling – coaching, therapy and personal development training. It's a pursuit that twenty years later still gives me a high.

From there I eventually found my way to writing self-help, life-coaching books, such as this one. These days as a semi-retiree I write, coach and run workshops helping people get their lives to work. I have found a passion, but remember *I wasn't born with it.*

It developed and blossomed from my experience and skills. It morphed and evolved and was not the result of a master plan.

You can see that over the years I developed skills in things I had an affinity for – but not a passion – to begin with. As my competence grew, my dedication and interest developed. *At every stage I built on skills and training I had already invested time and money in.* Even the library sidetrack increased my confidence and gave me skills in reading aloud to groups of people.

If I look at my story, I can see patterns emerging; a love of learning just for the sake of it, some interpersonal skills, confidence in standing up in front of a group and teaching and training. There are some skills in there worth pursuing, i.e. skills that don't come naturally to everyone.

Lest this sound like I'm bragging, there is also a humbling and contrasting pattern of laziness and unwillingness to go deep into a subject *unless* I'm convinced it has a practical value for me or is exciting and entertaining. If a subject doesn't turn me on, I will simply ignore it. Hence I know a little about a lot of things.

But once I determine that something might be useful to me I get manic. I got wired about NLP and hypnotherapy. I was obsessive about what makes a good sales person. I'm addicted to helping people find life purpose. These skills are hardly chemical engineering or law, but hey, I'm having fun.

That's my story. I want you to write yours.

Building on innate talents and trained skills

As Cal Newport suggests, using your skills, plus your experience, plus your natural affinities, is an intensely satisfying way to progress. I'm not saying everyone should persist with this. I know a number of

Chemical Engineers who have nothing to do with chemical engineering. Not to mention Librarians who never enter a library.

If you find your education and training is in something you absolutely detest, then by all means, follow something different. Get on a new trail. Your skill set is important, but no one is suggesting you plod along with something you hate simply because you have the training. I haven't set foot in a library for thirty years.

But I think you will discover, that on looking back, nothing you learn or experience needs to be wasted. I got a lot from my few years among the bookshelves, even if it wasn't my dream career. For one thing, I learned the discipline of getting up every morning and going to a job I had no interest in. That served me later on a number of occasions. Sometimes we just have to grit our teeth and do something we don't like if it serves a higher good, in this case a regular paycheck.

Just to recap, Cal Newport was not arguing *against* having passion for what you do; he argues against the strategy of going for what you love *first* and assuming bliss and a sense of fulfilling purpose will follow. He says that is bad strategy.

He very much wants people to end up loving what they are doing, but believes that going for passion first won't get you there. He propounds the necessity of getting good at something and then watching the passion follow.

Passion grows with skill.

This is the strategy most of us would benefit from…unless we are a Mozart or Picasso.

Your task for now: read these questions, think about them and use them to get you started on your timeline.

What have you always been good at?

What talents do you have?

What are you trained in?

What subjects in school were easy for you?

What jobs did you excel at?

What challenges have you overcome in life?

What wounds, psychological or physical, have you overcome and healed?

Now write your story using a timeline. Use mine as an example. Examine it. What are the patterns? What keeps turning up?

We are going to look at persistent interests and patterns, learn from them and then pool them with some other ideas gathered in this book. There's a lot more to come.

Coaching question:

There is something you can do better than anyone else because they are not you. What is it?

Chapter 6

Your Mission, Should You Choose to Accept It: Follow Your Bliss

"Follow your bliss.
If you do follow your bliss,
you put yourself on a kind of track
that has been there all the while waiting for you,
and the life you ought to be living
is the one you are living...
If you follow your bliss,
doors will open for you that wouldn't have opened for anyone else."
– Joseph Campbell

"I just don't know what to do with my life!" wailed Suzanne, my client, a lady in her late 50s who had just retired from a high flying sales and marketing position for a well-known shoe company. She had recently moved to San Miguel de Allende in central Mexico, from the States and was feeling frustrated that she wasn't having as much fun as she had anticipated.

"I'm a bit bored to be honest. I guess I wasn't ready to retire completely, because I don't have anything to do. I worked all my life for a big company. Now I'm feeling at loose ends, but I really don't want to go back to corporate life and full time work. Not at all. But what can I do here when I've been in sales and marketing all my life? It's not like I'm a healer or something easily transferable to another situation.

"I feel kind of useless, after years of feeling successful."

This was right up my alley. "*Wait,*" I said. *"You've got loads of skills you're just not recognizing. What made you good at your job? What skills did you learn? What was your favorite bit of work?"*

She was easily able to answer these questions. She obviously had marketing skills, but also organizing skills and keeping to a budget with her eye on the bottom line at all times, i.e. making a profit. These were all rare and valuable skills she had garnered through the years.

We spent quite a while stockpiling her arsenal of abilities, identifying natural talents and pulling in all her training courses. We built up a picture of a smart and accomplished lady.

"But how do I use any of that now?" she moaned.

"Wait, I'm not done with you," I promised.

"Now comes the fun part. What do you love doing? Forget about a career or anything restricting your response. What do you really love?" I pressed her for answers.

She paused for a moment. "*Oh,"* she said. "*I hadn't thought of this before, but my favorite part of the job was styling people, either clients or models, for advertising events. I just loved it. I love to style my friends, help them find the right clothes for the least amount of money and I can make them look terrific. So much fun! Plus I'm good at it. Being in the fashion industry for so many years, I just absorbed a lot of know-how unconsciously. I guess you could say I'm an expert."* She laughed at her own words.

"I never thought of this before!" She repeated in awe.

Ok! Here we go! *"What I have observed,"* I began, *"is that in San Miguel there are lots of people with talents and passions similar to your love of styling. However, what they lack are skills in running a business. So although many would love to create a little styling money-spinner of their own, their passion never gets off the ground and is frequently dead on arrival. They don't have a clue how to market their skills or their passions or set up a business. Many lose a lot of investment money.*

"You however, have all those skills in spades. You would know how to assess the market, how to reach your demographic and how to make it work as a business. You have all the entrepreneurial skills in the world! You could really get it to work for you. A styling business."

"Yes!" she said. *"Makeovers, weddings, special events! Yes, yes, yes! What fun! I would know exactly what to do! I love helping people feel good about themselves. It gives me a buzz!"*

What do you love?

Remember when Malcolm Gladwell says to *pursue what interests you. Not what you're good at?* And then goes on to say that passion gets you further than some *dry notion of ability*?

This sounds like a total contradiction to the ideas of Cal Newport we discussed in the last chapter. Cal wants you to start with what you already can do well. At first glance pursuing passion sounds like a lot more fun and definitely more modern and *today* than simply sticking with what you can already do.

Follow your bliss. Does this sound better than: go take a course in something you can already do. Get better at it. Practice for 10,000 hours?

It does. But let's examine further.

Hmm…I love cats

Passionately. Does this mean I should find a career with cats or that they are my life purpose? I don't think so somehow. Kitties are fabulous creatures and I adore them. But I don't really think I should be doing any more than putting down kibble and the frequent cuddle. My skills in cat care don't go much beyond this.

But trust me on this: If I did want to open some sort of business around cats, no matter how much business savvy I had, if I didn't have a *love* of cats, it would not work. There are two sides to this coin.

Looking at Cal and Malcolm, it's obvious we need both qualities in our lives – skill and passion – to really find that perfect compelling self-expression. We have determined that we need skills. But equally important, without passion, or a love, intense interest and excitement for doing something, you won't do it for long, no matter how qualified, experienced and talented you are. You must *want* to do it.

Crave it, die for it, intensely need-to-do-it passion. Bliss.

> *"I do know what bliss is: that deep sense of being present, of doing what you absolutely must do to be yourself."*
> *– Joseph Campbell*

Discovering your passion should be easy, but it's surprising how many people claim they don't know what they really want to do. *Well if I really had a passion for something, finding my purpose would be easy, right?*

Sometimes it isn't so painless and simple. We cover up our passions, our compelling interests, because we are led to believe we can't make a living at them, or they are superficial, or are not worthy of attention. *That's a great hobby*, we are told.

FOLLOW THE TRAIL OF YOUR SPIRIT

Some of us have never given ourselves time to explore what we really love or want to do. It seems like fantasy, irresponsible. So let's indulge in a little daydreaming in this chapter. Nothing is set in stone and no one will laugh at you or dismiss your reveries, because you're not going to tell anyone! Not just yet, anyway.

Ponder these questions:

- What excites you? Floats your boat? Gives you most joy?
- What activity in your life makes you feel like this is what you were born to do?
- How would you choose to spend your time if you were totally free from responsibilities? (No job, family, financial, or health constraints.)
- What gets you in ***flow***, i.e. so absorbed you lose all sense of time and place? That makes you feel hyped up and energetic after hours of doing it? (Mine is standing in front of a group sermonizing. Yours may be sports, art, music, gardening.)
- Everyone is willing to spend money and be a bit indulgent in some area. What would you pay money to do? What activities are you willing to spend a good amount of money on that would cause someone else to pause? (Workshop in Sedona? Ayahuasca retreat in Peru? Travel to exotic locations? Expensive healers? An MBA from Stanford? A trip to Tibet to study Buddhism? A commercial pilot's license?)
- What have you spent, overall, the most ***time*** on through the years? (Let's leave out TV or playing on the computer. Living alone in a forest? Reading? Sailing? Work?)

- **If you could do a workshop** anywhere in the world, on any subject, money no object, where and what would it be?
- **If you could go on a trip** somewhere, anywhere in the world, all expenses paid and join in an activity there, what and where would it be?

Answer the above questions as best you can. Skip ones that don't grab you. I'll wait. What you may find is you have more than one passion. All the better to work with, my dear.

My experiences, again

I know, I know – me, me, me. But I'm hoping my experiences may trigger something in you.

I have come upon these passion questions at various times in my life. Sometimes they made sense and other times they didn't. But each question brought me closer to realizing what I love doing and what I am deep down passionate about. It was never clear-cut like *I want to be a concert pianist* or *I want to be an actress*. I never felt compelled towards a career of any type. Yet here I am, past the age of retirement, doing work I love that brings me great satisfaction.

I'm what you would call a *late bloomer*. A blooming boomer! A late blooming boomer...

Check out these clues and patterns.

In every job I had whether in libraries, real estate, or recruitment, **I loved sitting down with people, talking to them, giving advice or help.** This eventually morphed into coaching and hypnotherapy, where it got more meaningful and intense.

People came to the library with queries and **I helped them find the answers and the books they needed.** I liked that. It was one of the few parts of the job I enjoyed.

I loved helping people find their perfect job when I took a brief stint in recruitment. (Notice what this book is about?)

I loved talking to people about what kind of house they wanted and matching it up with what I was selling, when I was working in real estate. What a buzz when I helped someone find his or her dream home! Closing a sale made me breathless.

But **my true passion is learning**. **New ideas really excite me** and I want to share them. I literally get up and pace around the room with excitement when I come upon a new idea in personal development. (Does this make me weird? Probably.)

My father always said he loved studying and reading because he knew he could share what he learned with his congregation and that gave him great satisfaction. I must have picked that up from him. I love sharing what I've learned with others in my coaching and writing.

I also like **teaching and training. I adore getting up in front of a group** and sharing information.

So when you combine my enjoyment of working with people one to one, helping and advising, plus my love of finding new ideas and sharing information, especially in front of groups, it's easy to see how I morphed into a coach and personal development trainer.

But when my own personal life coach really pushed me about what I love doing most, I realized it was writing. This came as a shock to me. But I became aware that writing pithy posts on Facebook gave me more joy than anything else I was doing. How sad is that? I would spend time on them, getting them right, crafting them.

Then I recalled that writing up training handouts was intensely satisfying to me and I loved designing courses and writing out the details.

Hmm. Maybe I should write something a little longer than a Facebook post? Would that be fun?

So I got started on articles, blogging and then books. I get to give advice, wanted or not, share my ideas and use writing skills gained in college, marketing, sales and designing training. I love it when people enjoy what I write, but I would do it anyway because I have a passion for it. It gets me in flow and I forget everything else. It's my ultimate creative self-expression.

I'm a late bloomer with many careers under my belt, with each one contributing to more satisfaction and use of skills than the one before. I'm not finished. Right now it's writing books, coaching, training. That will undoubtedly transmute into something else. That's what following the trail of your spirit is all about. The trail keeps on going.

What about you? What do you love to do? How do you like to express yourself?

Your mission: Write down the answers to the questions at the beginning of the chapter. Here they are again:

- What excites you? Floats your boat? Gives you most joy?
- What activity in your life makes you feel like this is what you were born to do?
- How would you choose to spend your time if you were totally free from responsibilities? (No job, family, financial, or health constraints.)

- What gets you in ***flow***, i.e. so absorbed you lose all sense of time and place? That makes you feel hyped up and energetic after hours of doing it? (Mine is standing in front of a group sermonizing. Yours may be sports, art, music, gardening.)
- Everyone is willing to spend ***money*** and be a bit indulgent in some area. **What would you pay money to do**? What activities are you willing to spend a good amount of money on that would cause someone else to pause? (Workshop in Sedona? Ayahuasca retreat in Peru? Travel to exotic locations? Expensive healers? An MBA from Stanford? A trip to Tibet to study Buddhism? A commercial pilot's license?)
- What have you spent, overall, the most ***time*** on through the years? (Let's leave out TV or playing on the computer. Living alone in a forest? Reading? Sailing? Work?)
- **If you could do a workshop** anywhere in the world, on any subject, money no object, where and what would it be?
- **If you could go on a trip** somewhere, anywhere in the world, all expenses paid and join in an activity there, what and where would it be?

Now look at what you have written. You will begin to identify what you love, what your passions are.

When you've got a picture and timeline of your interests and experiences you can start to identify patterns. What has always been a theme with you in what you like to do? Like me with my love of interviewing and helping people one on one? Or my love of getting up in front of groups? What have you always enjoyed?

"You are what your deep, driving desire is.
As your desire is, so is your will.
As your will is, so is your deed.
As your deed is, so is your destiny." – Upanishads

Now you have identified your skills and talents, natural abilities. You are also uncovering what you really love to do. Can you match them up? What comes to mind? Are ideas for what you could do that you would both love to do AND be good at starting to form?

We will develop this and help you find your destiny. But there is another piece to the love and skills bit that I want to introduce you to. This next chapter will help you identify both. Curious? It's a really important signpost. Read on…

Coaching question:

What would you do if you knew you couldn't fail?

Chapter 7

Archetypes - Discovering Your True Self

"Your vision will become clear only when you can look into your own heart. Who looks outside, dreams; who looks inside, awakes." – Carl Jung

Are there repeating patterns in your life? Do the same people keep showing up in different bodies? Do you always end up with no money? Have accidents? Land on your feet? Seem to have a guardian angel?

Maybe it has occurred to you that nothing is accidental and that these patterns are there for a reason.

Here we are, reading the signposts that will keep you on the trail of your spirit. You still may not be sure what you want to do with your life but I trust you are becoming more aware of what makes you tick. You've enumerated your skills, natural talents and abilities, plus your education and experiences. You've probably got a good grasp of things you love to do.

But there still may be a few missing pieces to the puzzle and I want to give you a little boost in understanding. Well, more like a rocket launcher. I think the following will help you gain some insight into who you are and what you love, plus what you naturally gravitate to doing.

Does that sound intriguing? I hope so! Because I'm going to share with you what has helped me *more than anything else* in understanding my own personality, values, propensities and why I do what I do.

I'm talking about discovering your *archetypes*: our character and individuality neatly wrapped up in metaphorical language.

Wait. Don't run off. This could be the most illuminating *and useful* bit of self-development you've ever come across. Have I sold you yet?

Soul Mates

I profess I love archetypes. I'm captivated by my own. They are like old friends, guides, soul mates, who have shaped me into the person I am today. They help me find my purpose, stick to my path and follow my bliss. And some get me in trouble.

Above all, they help me stay on the trail and not stray too far from the main pathway.

The woo-woo version

Now, if for a moment I can be esoteric about this, here goes: archetypes are primordial (age-old) spiritual beings that operate in you and form your character and to a great extent dictate your personality. I say spiritual because they don't exist literally, but metaphorically. There's an aura of the mystical to them.

Carl Jung, the great Swiss psychiatrist and psychoanalyst, first used the term *archetype* to signify ancient patterns of personality that appear in the world's myths, legends and folk tales. He referred to them as the shared heritage of the human race that resides in what he called the "collective unconscious."

He goes on to say,

> *"The primordial image, or archetype, is a figure – be it a daemon, a human being, or a process, that constantly recurs in the course of history...Essentially, therefore, it is a mythological figure..."*

If all this sounds similar to astrology, or the Enneagram, that's because it is. All of the personality styles, Myers-Briggs, Jung, Tarot cards, spirit guides, angels, the personas in the Zodiac and Greek myths and legends – all are referring to archetypal characters. The ones of interest here are those that shape your personality and influence your likes and dislikes.

A more down to earth explanation

Now if I want to be more prosaic, rather than esoteric, I would put it like this: you, as an individual, are an interesting mix of values, beliefs, opinions and personality traits. Some you have picked up along the way, been taught by your elders, or figured out for yourself and others you seem to have been born with.

Those personality traits you were born with we call archetypes, because they are shared by all of humanity since the dawn of time. Archetypal. We shape them into mythological characters in order to understand them better.

Did your mom say you always were a pest? Or a little angel? Or that you were a sweetheart? (no, nor mine). My mother laughingly said I came out mad and complaining – my Rebel archetype testing its lungs – and that it turned out to be a very accurate forewarning of my personality. (Don't worry, she liked me anyway.)

I'm still the same, although many decades and tons of personal development work have toned down the excesses. And even though I've learned how to behave, the basic character is still there. I wouldn't want to get rid of my *Rebel* entirely!

Now in the same way that values are basically good, but can be corrupted to the other extreme, so can archetypes. There are no bad archetypes, not even the *Rebel*, but they all do have a shadow side if natural tendencies are not kept in check. And that usually is a life theme for most of us – how to keep our shadows in the shadow and not trampling over relationships and everything we hold dear.

We study archetypes for their use and not to victimize. Most people find life easier if they don't attempt to repress an archetype, but rather work with it. That's what I want to show you how to do.

Mysteries unveiled

Joseph Goldstein, in *Insight Meditation,* says it well,

> *" A healthy sense of self develops through learning to see clearly and accept all the difficult parts of who we are."*

Your archetypes can help you understand things about yourself that before may have been a conundrum – your tastes, life choices, friends, skills and temperament, even the clothes you wear and how you decorate your living space.

Most importantly, for the purposes of this book, they help you become more aware of your likes, dislikes and innate preferences for activities and careers.

Archetypes can spell out your purpose to you in ten-foot high letters – if you pay attention to them.

My *Seeker* archetype made me realize I needed to incorporate study, learning and the quest for wisdom in any purpose or calling I pursued. I thrive on new insights – like a drug addiction without the side effects.

You know who you are

Examples of archetypes are King, Queen, Hero, Artist, Actor, Rebel, Free Spirit, Seeker, Scientist, Damsel in Distress, Warrior, Witch – the list is endless.

I bet you resonated with at least one or two on that list, thinking, hey ho, that's me! They are so much a part of us that we recognize them immediately.

When I refer to your archetypes I am talking about just that – those that resonate with you and feel like old friends. Soul mates.

Call someone a witch and many will take it as an insult; call someone with a Witch archetype a witch and she will nod agreeably. I have a friend, a nice sweet lady, who purrs with pleasure when I call her a Witch. I share her secret.

Call me a Warrior, Adventuress, Rebel, or An Old Hippie at Heart and I puff up with pride. Yes! Many would not like those labels. My sister is one of them. She can't for the life of her understand why anyone would want to be called a hippie. But call me a Caregiver, Rescuer, Angel, or Domestic Goddess and I will look bewildered. It ain't me, babe.

So what is the point of all this and how does it relate to finding life purpose?

Just this. Identifying and understanding your archetypes and how they operate in your life will explain ALL of this. It will help you understand why you are attracted to certain people, careers, training, education, partners and can point you in the right direction to *keep on truckin'* on the trail of your spirit.

You can change, develop, mature, evolve and you can choose to work with your archetypes or to fight them. But if you try to repress them it can be the cause of depression or getting stuck – mental and emotional paralysis.

We all the know the (archetypal) story of a young artist or musician coerced by his parents into banking or accounting and how miserable and frustrating his life can become.

We are all the same; try and force us into something to which we're not suited and we wilt on the vine.

What Plato says

Plato would opine that prior to this lifetime you made an agreement with everyone who shows up in your life, in order to learn certain lessons and fulfill certain obligations. (I threw Plato in because he gives the whole archetype shebang credibility.)

And Plato really did say it, in *The Republic*. He wrote that every human soul makes a pre-birth contract, or agrees to a reincarnation, or journey to undertake, with a soul group and chooses the life it thinks will help the most on this journey. I consider an idea like this metaphorical, not literal, and illustrating an internal truth. But oh, don't you agree it's an interesting one?

Each archetype has a reason to be in your life, a contract you need to honor. Each has a lesson to teach that helps you find your path and true purpose. And as you begin to understand yourself better, you have more chance of living a fulfilling and exciting life.

My archetypes got me on track and enabled me to create the life I was craving; more me, more speaking with my authentic voice, more aligned and sure of myself. *Margaret Unleashed*, as my *Peacemaker* non-hippie sister somewhat warily describes it.

Characteristics of archetypes

Here are a few characteristics of archetypes, to give you their flavor.

Ancient

Legendary

Arcane

Timeless

Mythological

Fabled

Classic

Universal

Tarot cards

Fairy tales

Astrology

Greek tragedies

Ancient gods/goddesses

We are born with them

They determine our individuality, our uniqueness

They are part of our soul – which is individualized spirit

All God figures in every religion are archetypes. God the Patriarch, the Loving Father, Divine Mother, Divine Lover (Krishna), Counselor, Comforter, Holy Ghost – all powerful archetypes.

Why we need to bring them into awareness

You cannot really serve or thrive or live your true purpose until you understand yourself, where you're coming from and where and how you can operate best.

For instance, whenever you hear people describe the difficult time they are having either professionally or personally you realize that many people are pursuing a life they are not suited for. They are repressing their archetypes and nothing can make that work.

Real pain comes from the desperation that we will never accomplish what we were meant to do in life. Deep in our unconscious, our spiritual potential lies in wait for us to release it.

When we bring our archetypes into conscious awareness we can start to unleash their incredible power and ability to transform our lives.

Now let's go find your archetypes. It's a trip. Really. Read on…

Coaching question:

If your life had a theme, or a lesson to learn, what would it be?

Chapter 8

Archetypes Exercise – Discovering Your Inner Circle

"It has always been the prime function of mythology and rite to supply the symbols that carry the human spirit forward, in counteraction to those that tend to tie it back."
– Joseph Campbell

This chapter is an assignment chapter. You will be working with deep mythological motifs. If you don't want to do the work just now, at least peruse the list of archetypes to become familiar with them. You may see some old friends.

Otherwise, notebooks out, please.

Here is a list of some of the most well known archetypes. It's by no means exhaustive. Have a look and make your own list of no more than 12 archetypes that strike you as familiar and feel a part of your psyche. Some may resonate with you more than others. That's ok. We call those our *inner circle.*

Just follow your heart, not your head – it's art, not science. Let go your thinking helmet and flow with it. It's pure fun (says this Adventuress) and you can't get it wrong.

The list is in part thanks to Caroline Myss and her book *Sacred Contracts*, where she really goes deeply into archetypes. Highly recommended. I originally learned about archetypes from her book.

Points to consider:

- Archetypes have a positive and a negative, or shadow, side. Both are listed here under these well known archetypes.
- The list includes a few predominantly Shadow archetypes because they are so familiar. Under these the Shadow side is listed first.
- There is some repetition, such as Guide and Shaman, Knight and Warrior, but there are slight differences and emphasis.

Archetypes – a list of some well known examples

Addict – Workaholic, Glutton, Shopaholic, Gambler
Shadow archetype. Obsessive focus on certain behaviors or substances, such as drugs, alcohol, nicotine or gambling. Willing to sacrifice close relationships, integrity, character, or emotional, spiritual and physical well being for it.

Shadow of the Workaholic, Gymnast, Athlete, Olympian or Sportsman, who become highly successful in their field and able to focus and channel their attention on something useful.

Activist – Advocate, Attorney, Social Crusader, Defender, Environmentalist
The Activist has a passion for defending the underdog and for justice and can become involved in controversial political concerns. Interested in changing the world and society.

The Shadow Activist can lose perspective and become a fanatic or in extreme cases a terrorist, losing sight of compassion and justice in pursuing the cause.

Artist – Musician, Author, Actor, Artisan, Sculptor
A passion for creative expression. The Artist is animated with the energy and compulsion to express it into physical forms.

The Shadow includes an eccentric nature and the madness that often accompanies genius, losing sight of practical day-to-day self-care. Jimi Hendrix, Jim Morrison, Vincent van Gogh.

Athlete – Olympian, Sportsman
This archetype represents the expression of the strength of the human spirit in the power of the human body. A code of ethics, discipline and morality is connected to this archetype, as is dedication to transcending the limits of physical form and the development of personal will power and strength of spirit.

The Shadow becomes obsessed with the sport to the detriment of health and well-being such as competitors who take harmful drugs to increase performance.

Child – Orphan, Wounded, Magical, Innocent, Nature, Divine, Eternal
The Child is a universal archetype and everyone has expressions of the Inner Child. The core issue of all the Child archetypes is dependency and responsibility. One of the above aspects of the Child is usually so dominant that it eclipses the energy of the others.

Child: Magical
The Magical Child represents the part of us that is both enchanted and enchanting and sees the potential for sacred beauty in all things. It also embodies the qualities of wisdom and courage in

the face of difficult circumstances. The Magical Child believes everything is possible. Michael Jackson was a Magical Child.

The Shadow manifests in pessimism and depression and a retreat into fantasy.

Child: Divine

The Divine Child is associated with innocence, purity and redemption qualities that suggest a special relationship with the Divine itself.

The Shadow manifests as an inability to defend itself against negative forces.

Child: Nature

A deep intimate bonding with natural forces and animals. Tender emotional qualities combined with a toughness and ability to survive. A life pattern of relating to animals in an intimate and caring way. Frequently cares more for nature than humans.

Child: Eternal

A determination to remain eternally young in body, mind and spirit. Age doesn't stop them from enjoying life with a healthy attitude.

The Shadow manifests as an inability to grow up and embrace responsibility. No foundation for a functioning adulthood. Peter Pan.

Clown – Comedian, Court Jester, Fool, Joker

The Clown is allowed to cross boundaries of social acceptance and is allowed into powerful circles. The Jester is the only one who can get away with making fun of the King. The Clown is able to see things as they are and to comment sharply on the hypocrisies of the day. Comedians on TV, in the press.

The Shadow manifests as cruel mockery or savage betrayal with the breaking of confidences.

Coach – Mentor, Role Model, Guide
Assists others to see things realistically; encourages, motivates, inspires.

Companion – Friend, Sidekick, Consort, Assistant, Secretary
Loyalty, tenacity and unselfishness often in support of a personality that has a stronger nature or role in life. Emotional support. Platonic friendship.

Damsel in Distress – Princess
Shadow archetype. The Damsel in Distress is beautiful and vulnerable and in need of rescue, specifically by a Knight, and once rescued is taken care of in lavish style. Helpless and in need of protection. Fear of going it alone. Associated with having a sense of entitlement and the belief that she is powerless without a Knight to protect her.

The Damsel is the shadow of the Princess who is powerful and independent and capable of taking care of herself.

Dilettante – Amateur, Dabbler
Someone who delights in and has an overall knowledge of a number of subjects but doesn't aspire to rise above the level of amateur. Loves the arts especially. Can be a critic, teacher, or commentator of arts or sports.

The Shadow manifests as a pretension to much deeper knowledge than actually possessed or not sufficient respect for those who practice the arts. Tendency to skim over subjects lightly or give viciously negative critiques.

Earth Mother – Caregiver, Nurturer, Rescuer

Life-giver, source of nurturing and nourishment, unconditional fountain of love, patience, devotion, caring and unselfish. Loves to care and look after others. Always reliable.

The Devouring, Abusive, Abandoning Mother represents the Shadow.

Empathic – Intuitive, Psychic

Someone with special sensitivities to the energies of others. Can be overwhelmed by crowds, negative people. Intuitive, psychic.

Shadow is the Vampire who sucks the energy of others, leaving them weakened.

Engineer – Architect, Builder, Designer, Organizer

Practical, hands-on, devoted to making things work. Grounded, orderly, strategic. Designs solutions to everyday problems.

Shadow can become obsessively detail oriented, to the exclusion of the big picture or vision.

Flirt

Charming, friendly, generally attractive to everyone. Highly refined skills at manipulating others without investing personal emotion. Easy to get others to do what they want.

Shadow drawn to money and power for the sake of personal control and survival. Not looking for a home in the suburbs. Femme Fatale, Black Widow, Seductress.

Free Spirit – Innocent, Hippie, Wild Child

Optimist, playful, fun-loving. Follows her heart, not her head. Flower Child, Hippie, Bohemian. Doesn't play by the rules but not especially rebellious.

Shadow can grow into the drug Addict, Outcast, Hermit, or Weirdo. Doesn't look after herself and suffers the consequences. Can end up homeless and broke.

God – Adonis

Great worldly power or great physical specimen, the ultimate in male dominance. Can be benevolent and compassionate, willing to use his powers to help others.

Shadow is a dictator or despot. You need to have sense of great power to claim this archetype.

Goddess

Fabulous woman. Source of all life, fertility, exaggerated sexual attributes. Can embody wisdom, guidance, physical grace, athletic prowess and sensuality. Sophia Loren.

Shadow can become the Diva, entitled and spoiled from too much attention.

Guide – Guru, Sage, Spiritual Master

Takes role of Teacher to spiritual level, teaching not only beliefs and practices of established religions, but also the principle of seeing the Divine in every aspect of life. Enjoys passing wisdom to others.

Shadow is the Guru who is interested in power, money and ego.

Healer – Intuitive, Therapist, Analyst, Doctor, Chiropractor

Passion to serve others in the form of repairing the body, mind and spirit.

Shadow can become drunk with power and control over the vulnerable.

Hedonist – Bon Vivant, Chef, Gourmet

An appetite for pleasurable aspects of life from good food and wine to sexuality and sensuality. Indulging the self is central to this archetype.

Shadow manifests as pursuing pleasure without regard for health or other people. Addiction to pornography, drugs, alcohol, or overweight is symptom of Shadow. Do not tend to age well, but become disillusioned and dissatisfied with pleasure and take it to extremes.

Innocent – Virgin

Pure, transparent, lacking underhanded intentions. Free Spirit, naive, optimist.

Shadow is the Cynic, disillusioned with betrayal.

Intellectual – Professor, Scholar, Academic

Rational, well read, scholarly, seeks knowledge and wisdom. Well informed. Well educated. Approaches life from a mental platform. Loves knowledge for the sake of it.

The Shadow can become more interested in cleverness than wisdom.

Judge – Critic, Mediator, Arbitrator

Interested in justice and law. Involved in interventions between people. Leads life of high standards and principles, and values a well-regulated society.

Shadow manifests destructive criticism, judgment without compassion or hidden agendas. Misuse of authority.

King – Emperor, Ruler, Chief, Godfather

Powerful and authoritative male. Benevolent and responsible. Likes to rule and exert control over his kingdom in return for leadership, stability, safety.

Shadow is the Tyrant, Dictator.

Knight – Hero, Rescuer, Warrior

Male associated with chivalry, courtly romance and protection of the Princess and going to battle for honorable causes.

Shadow has the power without honor and chivalry – Mercenary, Gun for Hire.

Lover

Loves passionately whether in romance, art, music, animals, gardening, poetry. A sense of unbridled and exaggerated affection and appreciation of someone or something that influences the organization of life and environment.

The Shadow manifests as an exaggerated, obsessive passion that has a destructive effect on one's physical or mental health – Addict, Stalker, Don Juan, Seductress, Black Widow.

Martyr

Suffering for the redemption of others. Dying for a cause.

Shadow manifests as the Victim. Self righteous, self-pitying. Poor me.

Missionary

Possesses absolute certainty about beliefs. No doubts or skepticism. Not looking for answers – has found them. Keen to share beliefs with any and everyone.

Shadow is fanatic who cares more about dogma than compassion.

Mystic – Renunciate, Hermit, Yogi

A fascination for the otherworldly, the spiritual, the arcane, the magical, the occult. Devoted to the spiritual path or to any great achievement that requires intense focus. Spiritual intensity, devotion, persistence, wisdom and single-minded dedication, relinquishing material desires and ambitions to pursue spiritual practice; can withdraw from the world to pursue the spiritual path or to pursue a solitary life.

Shadow is overly pious or privileged, or reclusive, not involved in the world – Troglodyte, grumpy Hermit.

Networker – Communicator, Messenger, Journalist
Great skill in bringing people together and making connections. Can forge alliances, champion causes, make things happen. Inspirational. Politician, Speaker of the House, Ronald Reagan.

Shadow is the Gossip, Society Journalist, Paparazzi.

Peacemaker – Mediator, Ambassador, Diplomat, Go-Between
Smooths over relations between antagonistic groups or individuals. Has patience and skill and an ability to read people and situations with great acuity. Respects both sides of an argument or cause. Lifelong commitment to resolving disputes and bringing people together.

Shadow can become wishy-washy and refuses to have an opinion. Two-faced and gutless.

Pioneer – Explorer, Settler, Hippie, Entrepreneur
Called to discover and explore new lands, whether internal or external. Passion to explore, initiate, innovate. A need to step onto fresh and undiscovered territory in at least one realm.

Shadow manifests as compulsive need to abandon one's past and move on to new conquests – Vagabond, Gypsy, Traveler, Homeless Person, Beggar.

Pirate – Swashbuckler, Robin Hood, Adventurer, Highwayman
Pirates were thieves of the open seas pursuing rich treasures and burying them in caves, creating legends around buried treasure

within the caves of our inner being. Symbolize freedom and ability to strike back at the wealthy and aristocratic. Rule breakers. Steal everything from intellectual property or information via the Internet. Wikileaks.

Shadow can go too far and hurt others. Killer or thief or criminal.

Poet

Combines lyricism with sharp insight finding the essence of beauty and truth in everything. In love with words.

Shadow is the Mad Poet, who will sacrifice everything for his art.

Priest /Priestess

Official capacity to make spiritual vows and perform rituals of initiation and ordination – commitment to religious authority. Conveys to the public the power of sacred teachings, rituals, wisdom and ethics of each spiritual tradition. Dedicated, committed to following established traditions.

Shadow is the Hypocrite, Child Abuser, TeleEvangelist, who doesn't walk his talk and abuses position of respect and power.

Prince

Royal but not the ruler in charge. Shows leadership, responsibility to the kingdom. Humanitarian. Compassionate and humble yet regal in bearing.

Shadow can have feelings of entitlement as an heir apparent who uses his position to advance himself. Spoiled or Lazy Prince thinks the world owes him a living without responsibility or needing to work for a living.

Princess

Female royal. Similar to Prince. Princess can be compassionate, caring for the poor, the destitute. Beautiful, generous spirited.

Shadow is Lazy Princess, entitled, doesn't want to support herself. Dependent on the King for support. Daddy's Little Princess.

Queen

Power and authority in a woman. Court can be company or home. Responsible, shows leadership, takes care of her subjects.

Shadow associated with arrogance and a defensive posture showing need to protect one's personal and emotional power. Can be lonely, cold and icy. Shadow Queens do not like challenges to their control, authority and leadership. Drama Queen.

Rebel – Non-conformist, Free Spirit, Iconoclast

Looks for the truth. May reject legitimate authority but craves honesty, justice and exposes hypocrisy. Looks for the spirit behind the law and refuses to accept establishment norms at face value.

Shadow is Rogue, Outcast, Misfit. Cynical and disruptive, violent revolutionary.

Rescuer – Fireman, Knight, Hero, Samaritan

Assists impersonally and professionally when needed and then withdraws. Provides an infusion of strength and support to help others survive a difficult situation, crisis or process.

Shadow becomes the Vigilante or hopes to forge an intimate, romantic bond with the one being rescued.

Seductress – Black Widow

Shadow archetype. Enchantress, Flirt, uses sexual attraction for power. Used to getting her way, manipulative. Strong survival instincts. Interested in men for what they can give her. Tends to consume and then abandon her love interests.

Shadow of the Lover. Angelina Jolie.

Seeker – Wanderer, Nomad, Explorer

One who searches for God or enlightenment. In search of wisdom and truth wherever it is to be found. Always interested in new paths, religions, teachers, wisdom literature.

The Shadow is the Lost Soul, on an aimless journey without direction, disconnected from goals and never finding answers.

Servant – Caretaker, Butler, Personal Assistant

Available to others for the benefit and enhancement of their lives. Likes to look after someone they can look up to who is successful or powerful. Chief of Staff, Lady in Waiting.

The Shadow is The Indentured Servant who sees himself bound by conditions of service that he cannot get out of, for example someone in an unhappy relationship who is waiting to get enough money to leave, to buy their freedom. Shadow also the Victim.

Shaman – Medicine Man, Witch, Sorcerer

Special abilities – magic, transformation, healing, psychic powers. Uses magic to cure illness, foretell the future, control the forces of nature. Relationship with the occult and with spiritual forces. Connection with nature, herbs, animals, spiritual guides.

Shadow is the Fake, the Pretender interested in followers and money and power.

Student – Disciple, Devotee, Follower

A pattern of constant learning, an openness to absorbing new information as an essential part of one's well-being. Loves learning anything new and will indulge in continuous education.

Shadow can show as Eternal Student who never embarks on the sea of life in earnest, but manages to find new reasons to continue being schooled without ever putting that knowledge to the test. Suggests an absence of mastery of any one subject but rather continual pursuit of intellectual development.

Teacher

Passion to communicate knowledge, experience, skill and wisdom. Loves a soapbox, classroom, audience.

Shadow more concerned with recognition than with imparting knowledge. Bullies or manipulates students.

Vampire – Black Widow

Shadow archetype. Drains the energy of others for his or her own psychic survival. Needy emotionally. A need for approval, a need to be taken care of and a fear of being abandoned. Co-dependent relationships. Seen in chronic complaining, gossip, over dependency, or holding onto relationships long after their sell by date.

Shadow of the Lover.

Victim

Shadow archetype. The poor-me syndrome, blaming others for problems or issues. Looks for sympathy or pity. Always sick. Always having accidents and looking for attention. Never taking personal responsibility for whatever happens.

Shadow of the Child or Martyr or Caregiver.

Warrior – Amazon, Soldier, Knight

Strong in both strength and spirit. Physical as well as psychic strength and the ability to protect, defend and fight for justice. Similar to Knight, but Knight is romantic. Warrior is invincible and loyal and carries out orders. The willingness to face challenges and fight battles with professional skill and detachment from emotion.

Women Warriors, Amazons, are fierce to defend their families and are loyal and brave on the field of battle.

Shadow is Mercenary, Gun for Hire.

Homework

Have you listed the archetypes that resonate with you? No more than 12 please. Now take your list and put a star by the one or ones that seem to describe you best. Indicate if the Shadow resonates more than the positive. (For me they are the *Rebel, Seeker, Teacher, Coach, Warrior, Adventuress, Eternal Student-shadow*.)

This is your inner circle of archetypes.

Take these ones through this questionnaire, one at a time.

1. Why did you feel attracted to this archetype?
2. Where and when have you seen it active in your life?
3. How did it influence your education?
4. Would your Mom/Dad/Siblings/other relative agree that this archetype embodies something essentially you?
5. What emotions does it inspire in you?
6. If this archetype had a message for you, what would it be?
7. What is it helping you to learn?
8. How have you noticed the Shadow operating in you?
9. What does this archetype tell you about your life purpose?

Now take each of your favorite archetypes through this process. I'll help you out here and use my favorite archetype, the *Seeker*.

The *Seeker* reflects my character the best. Followed closely by *Rebel/Brat.*

Name: The *Seeker* – related archetypes *Wanderer, Vagabond, Nomad*

Description: The *Seeker* is one is always seeking for wisdom, God, spiritual enlightenment and *aha!* moments. The *Seeker* is interested in digging up the truth, no matter where it can be found and is not necessarily tied to any religion or organized spiritual path.

Seekers are obsessively interested in new ideas and learning is their greatest joy.

The *Seeker* typically buys every new book on a given subject, goes to every workshop or seminar and is passionately interested in trying new therapies or learning from new teachers.

- Why did you feel attracted to this archetype?

  Me: Always looking for new ideas, theories and personal development techniques.

  Will go on the drop of a hat to seminars on the other side of the world if they promise enlightenment or at the very least, new perspectives.

- Where and when have you seen it active in your life?
- How did it influence your education?

  I loved education when young and study continuously today. My BA degree is in Religion and Philosophy.

- Would your Mom/Dad/Siblings/other relative agree that this archetype embodies something essentially you?

  Yes. Always off on some new adventure.

- What emotions does it inspire in you?

  Nothing excites me more than learning new ideas that further my personal and spiritual development.

- If this archetype had a message for you, what would it be?
- What is it helping you to learn?

  To gain certitude, to be sure, to know without doubt.

  Message: To settle, to learn to trust, to have faith. To believe in something

- How have you noticed the Shadow operating in you?

  The *Lost Soul* – someone who can't settle with any one system of ideas, anywhere and who is disconnected and ungrounded. A bit bewildered.

  I can be that way. I sometimes put down a book with all the answers I need and think – Next! I go on an expensive course and as soon as it's over, immediately forget all about it. I keep looking and never find for certain. There's always something new on the horizon I need to check out first.

- What does this archetype tell you about your life purpose?

  I need a purpose that includes study and search. Writing books and running workshops entail research and really digging into a subject. It's good for me because it forces me to focus and not just skim the surface.

> It is my passion and my love and I have skills and education that back up my *Seeker*. It is a natural inclination. Writing and workshops and coaching are perfect channels for learning new ideas and sharing them.

Are you a *Seeker*? Do you thirst and crave for new ideas, for truth, for wisdom? Does a new insight give you the greatest buzz possible? If so, then think about what this means for you in your life search for purpose, career and meaning. How can you channel your *Seeker* obsessions into something useful and satisfying?

The Shadow in every archetype always gives us lessons we need. We must be aware of the pitfalls of the Shadow side of our favorite archetypes and be watchful and alert. The Shadow holds the secret to success. Overcoming our Shadows makes us strong and resilient.

You may begin to notice that many archetypes overlap. That's fine. Just find the ones that express an aspect of you. It doesn't have to be totally you.

Ok, now hang onto this list. We're going to use it for the next step.

But first! Don't forget to download your printable PDF version of the archetypes list in this chapter that you can work on when finding your archetypes.

www.margaretnashcoach.com/free

Coaching question:

Which archetype really excites your soul? What does this archetype tell you about your life purpose?

Chapter 9

Meaning and Significance

"Hear O children of immortal bliss! You are born to be united with the lord. Follow the path of the illumined ones, And be united with the Lord of Life." – Upanishads

This is one of my all time favorite quotes and I love to repeat it every morning before my meditation. For me it kind of says it all. It's got such a glorious ring to it, triumphant and clear, like a trumpet sounding. It's quite definite about the meaning of life.

In the quest for life purpose, the real goal is finding meaningful work, whether you are retired, semi-retired, just starting your work life or doing unpaid service or art of some sort. This book is predicated on the assumption that you want to find activity and work that have significance.

Let's recap – The three criteria for purposeful work are:

1. Are you any good at it?
2. Do you love it?
3. Does it have meaning and significance for you?

I think to understand if your work has meaning, it's important to uncover *your definition of the meaning of life.* We need to distinguish between the meaning of all life versus your individual purpose in life. They are different, but should be aligned for perfect self–expression.

Follow me down this rabbit hole

So what is my favorite quote saying? Let's unpack it to find its meaning. I studied theology in college, so I love exegesis (explanation of text). Please indulge me.

Go back up and reread it, please.

For one, it's calling Universal Spirit, God, the Universe, or Brahman, whatever name you like to use, *immortal bliss.* Now I don't know about you, but I find this definition rather appealing and it has the added advantage of no negative connotations attached to it.

It says we are the children of this bliss, so we are in essence bliss. Again, hard to object to. Pretty darned attractive.

Then it gives a clear statement as to why we are here – to be united with this bliss. I confess I don't know what that means, to be united with the lord, with bliss, but it sounds nice and I'd probably like to go there.

Then – and this is what I love – it tells us how to go about this in one easy sentence fragment: "*Follow the path of the illumined ones"*…Wait, who are they?

Illumined means full of light, enlightened, so I'm assuming it refers to spiritual masters and enlightened teachers. And it doesn't say follow just one, it says *ones*, so it's not limiting you to any one path. It implies there are lots of them, from Buddha to Jesus to Yogananda to the Dalai Lama. Take your pick. It doesn't distinguish between them.

If you have a Seeker archetype like I do, you'll want to study all of them. I guess why I like this quote is that it seems to be saying, *hey, you're OK for exploring as many as you can find. "Illumined ones*." Plural. I'm good.

And one last point; it says follow the *'path'* of the illumined ones, not follow the illumined ones. Follow their path. So we can follow what they teach us, the direction they point us in. We don't have to join anything, or pledge any commitment to an organization. Just find one of these illumined beings and get on the path. Get with the program. Or follow your spirit trail, like the Hopi Shaman recommends.

I love it. This works for me, although I'm not sure what grade my old college professor would give for that interpretation.

What works for you? What resonates with your very being so that you jump out of the chair like I did when I first read this quoted verse? What feels right to you in your very core?

It's so easy to find illumined beings and their paths these days. Within minutes, on your favorite technological toy of choice, you can download the *Dhammapada*, the *Bhagavad Gita,* the *Sermon on the Mount, the Kaballah, The Tibetan Book of the Dead,* or the *Tao Te Ching and* be immersed in the most revered ancient wisdom ever produced by mankind – from time immemorial.

Some religions teach that our purpose here is to evolve and learn and that life is simply one big school. Others claim we have many lives and that each has a lesson for us that will help us in the next life as we slowly move towards Nirvana or Heaven or Oneness.

We find teachings that say we can only take our virtues with us to the next stage of existence so our purpose is to develop those virtues.

Or maybe you've always been taught that we have one life to live and we need to get it right, or else…something. Karma, the result of your actions, will eventually come home to bite. Does this work for you?

Some believe there is no purpose to life.

Stephen Hawking, the great and legendary physicist, says:

> *"I believe the simplest explanation is, there is no God. No one created the universe and no one directs our fate. This leads me to a profound realization that there probably is no heaven and no afterlife either. We have this one life to appreciate the grand design of the universe and for that, I am extremely grateful."*

What is your take on the meaning of life?

Complete this sentence: *Life is like…*

An exciting journey? A learning experience? A school for personal growth? An opportunity to develop soul enhancing qualities? A testing ground? A vale of tears? (hope not!) A series of challenges to overcome that will make you stronger or kill you? A battleground? A tale told by an idiot? A dream?

Your sentence will almost certainly be different from the person sitting next to you. That's OK. I would venture to say no two people have the same definition of the purpose or meaning of life.

I think I would say life is like an exciting journey, a learning experience and a school for developing good qualities. I also believe that our job is getting our lives to work: It's as if we've been given this body, this personality, the situation we are born into and told, *here, make this work. Let's see what you do with it.*

That means I gravitate towards new learning opportunities (because that's what life is all about, right?), adventures, challenges and anything that makes me smarter and wiser. I also love helping people get their lives to work.

Discovering what you believe is the meaning of life is going to help you find your individual purpose.

Here are some favorite and well-known interpretations of the meaning of life. See if any resonate with you.

Do you love the vision of these poets and seers:

"All of life is a magical adventure – the most magical of all adventures is the ascent to and the expression of higher consciousness – it is the very purpose of life."
– In the Valley of Supreme Masters

"The task of the human spirit on earth is to purify its heart to enable it to see through the veil and focus on the spiritual realm. The heart must pierce the mystery of this life and see the beginning and the end with unclouded vision." – Rumi

Or maybe:

"Our birth is but a sleep and a forgetting:
The Soul that rises with us, our life's Star,
Hath had elsewhere its setting,
And cometh from afar:
Not in entire forgetfulness,
And not in utter nakedness,
But trailing clouds of glory do we come
From God, who is our home."
– William Wordsworth

Or deep down do you really feel Shakespeare had it pegged?

"Out, out, brief candle!
Life's but a walking shadow, a poor player,
That struts and frets his hour upon the stage,
And then is heard no more.
It is a tale
Told by an idiot, full of sound and fury,
Signifying nothing."

Peruse these questions and answer those that intrigue you:

1. What were you taught as a child was the meaning of life, the purpose of being here?
2. In what, if any spiritual tradition, were you brought up?
3. What is that tradition's version of the meaning of life?
4. Do you agree with it? Have you adopted another view? If so what is it?
5. If you don't know, or don't really have a belief around this subject, what would be one that would be most empowering to you? What gives you a good feeling about life?

Maybe you haven't thought about this before. Just play around with it. It does have bearing on what you will decide is meaningful activity. So let's move on to exploring your personal purpose of life, one that aligns with your belief in the meaning of life.

Values are key

Closely involved in your interpretation of the meaning of life, are your values. A value is what is important to you. Some would say it is what informs our attitudes toward life.

Here is a list of values, by no means conclusive:

Integrity

Justice

Love

Family

Friendship

Authenticity

Freedom

Independence

Creativity

Spirituality

Compassion

Caring for others

Achievement

Advancement

Competition

Winning

Creating a legacy

Purity of heart

Caring for nature

Caring for animals

Making a difference

Creating change

Inspiring and motivating others

Making money

Teaching

Learning

Personal development

Spiritual development

Serving God

Serving man

Doing my best

Peace

Unity

Bliss

The list is endless. These are some of the most common values in western societies. In eastern cultures you might find a different emphasis, with entries like serving society, humility, putting others before oneself, serenity, acceptance, co-operation.

Pick some from the list that you feel are important to you and feel free to add your own. Be honest. Nobody else needs to see this.

The ones that resonate with you and that you take for granted are what we call *core values* – our deepest seated beliefs. You feel like everyone surely must share those values because they are so obvious. You might be very surprised. I know it's a cliché, but we are all so different.

Most core values are instilled in us at a very early age, before we are seven. Before seven we are not capable of discrimination and tend to accept whatever we are taught by our elders. It's what we *have been brought up to believe* and very hard to shift.

It's important to recognize your core values, because some may not be authentic to whom you are now. For instance, I rejected the belief, as I grew older, that Christianity was the only true religion and everyone else was doomed (exclusivity). This never made sense to me (I used to worry about the Hindus!) and as I got older I embraced Universalism, the idea that there are many paths to truth. Interesting that this is a fundamental Hindu teaching.

I like this:

"That each tribe or nation should have its own particular God and think that every other is wrong is a superstition that should belong in the past." – *Vivekananda*

Hence Universalism is a *new* core value for me. Universalism has become more mainstream these days and the belief in exclusivity not so popular. Nevertheless many hold the idea, some because it was installed at an early age.

This has a huge influence on how I live my life, what activities I participate in, what organizations I join and whom I choose for friends and life partners. Your core values are impacting your life choices in ways you're probably not even aware of.

Because of my values of universalism, continuous learning, freedom and authenticity, I feel like a bird in a cage if I'm tied to any system of thought or belief that tells me how I must think.

From my Calvinist Protestant background come the "Protestant ethic" values of self-reliance, independence, hard work, a guilty conscience about…just about everything, but especially laziness. This means I am a bit driven to be productive and achieving and I always want to be earning my own money, having my own business and staying active until I pass on to the next stage of the journey. This so-called *Protestant* ethic is found in almost every society and culture in some form.

You may have been brought up to believe in competition and achievement, which will show itself in your work life, or you may have been taught that advancing yourself is wrong, so you gravitate towards charity or service work. Many feel guilty about earning too much money. This is almost always a sign of a core value asserting itself.

When I moved to England in my early twenties I was shocked that so many Brits came across as self-effacing. Competition, being successful, achievement and especially blowing your own horn, were frequently looked down on as being 'American' and somehow not cool. I took advantage of it because I wasn't hindered at all in that respect.

When values collide

Frequently core values *seem* to conflict with one another. You notice this when you feel uneasy about an action you have taken, or unsure what you think about an issue or problem. You (metaphorically) feel conflicted, carrying on arguments in your head.

Perhaps you feel inauthentic, frustrated with your own behavior, or incongruent. This is a sure sign some value is being trampled on and you're not being true to yourself.

Values don't actually conflict however. They can become *corrupted.* For example, the value of justice can become corrupted to fanaticism, achievement to ruthless competition, family loyalty to blind tribalism, speaking your truth to hurtfulness, protecting nature to environmental terrorism. So when values seem to conflict, it's usually because one is corrupted.

If values are pure then they work together to form a whole. Competition can work alongside co-operation if both values are clean. Patriotism can work alongside globalism, the need for peace of mind alongside activism.

So whether you resonate with Paul McCartney and his entreaty to *Let It Be*, or Mick Jagger's *Street Fighting Man*, there is no need for conflict as long as the values stay honest and balanced.

Answer these questions and add them to your archetypes:

What are your top five core values?

How do you see them evident in your life choices?

Do you notice any conflicts? Where and when? How do you resolve them?

When do you feel inauthentic? Why?

Now keep this list and answers. It's going to form an important part of your new story and help you formulate your mission.

Coaching question:

When are the times when you've felt most authentic, most aligned? What were you up to?

Chapter 10

Crafting Your Mission Statement

"People say that what we're all seeking is a meaning for life. I don't think that's what we're really seeking. I think that what we're seeking is an experience of being alive...so that we actually feel the rapture of being alive."
– Joseph Campbell

What makes you feel the rapture of being alive?

We have looked at what you believe is the purpose of life, all life. We have identified your values, those core beliefs and attitudes that make you who you are.

As Eckhart Tolle says, your inner purpose is to awaken and your outer purpose is unique to you, is what you do and it can change over time.

"Finding and living in alignment with the inner purpose is the foundation for fulfilling your outer purpose. It is the basis for true success."

Now it's time to look at your mission, i.e. your unique, individual, outer purpose for being here.

The idea behind having a mission is that each one of us has something unique to bring to the party, something nobody else can contribute, because they are not you. This is your personal statement, the one that will inform what you do with your time and what activities have value for you.

Life Purpose Coach Tim Kelley says,

> *"Imagine for a moment that all the really significant things that have happened in your life, your major relationships, job changes, significant crises and accidents, were intentional...*
>
> *...imagine that you have been training your whole life for something, for some significant task or job. Every major event in your life has made you better prepared for this purpose.*
>
> *What job does this resumé prepare you for? It is a unique position and you are the only one qualified for it!"*

This last question helped me more than almost any other I came across in my life purpose search. Before that I had thought in terms of my limitations, how I wasn't as good or qualified as others in certain areas. This question forced me to think what I had to offer – and to whom – that no one else had.

It came as a liberating shock to realize that no one else shares my unique experiences, background, friends, parents, or situation in life and no one else has overcome the same problems I have encountered in exactly the same way.

And the same applies to you.

So everyone's take on problem solving or facing difficulties will be different. Someone out there will resonate with what you have to offer and the way you offer it. I guess that means there's always room for one more book, one more painting and another coach in town. There's room for you and what you have to offer counts to someone. It doesn't matter what other people do. You count.

Does that feel good, or what?

Ask yourself these questions about your chosen activities:

Am I using my skills and innate talents?

Am I doing something I love?

Do I have a vision?

Does it align with my values and is it creative self-expression?

Can I take my creative work that I love and am good at and make it significant?

This last question is not as difficult to answer as it sounds. If you have found something you are good at doing and that you love, you can find how to make it align with your values and be meaningful.

Everything you do can have value.

I want you to create your own mission statement about your life – for right now, not for the past and not necessarily for the future – that describes the value and meaning of what you are doing.

Your unique mission is about *expressing who you are in life.* It's about expressing your attitudes, beliefs and values.

The attitude of gratitude

As a life-coach I like things that work, that get results and help people make useful changes in their everyday lives. And I'm especially impressed by how well one practice seems to work in shifting a self-pitying or complaining attitude into a more positive one.

I'm talking about the practice of gratitude: that is, writing or focusing on what you are grateful for in your life, rather than paying attention to what is going wrong. The attitude of gratitude seems to trump all others and when you are feeling grateful you cannot simultaneously feel resentful, angry, or sorry for yourself.

Kudos to it. It is an important point to remember and does seem to help many feel better about themselves and able to cope with whatever life throws in their path.

However, sometimes I find myself, like the proverbial stubborn mule, balking at the word itself. I just don't like the word gratitude very much and I think I know why. I'm sorry. I know this borders on sacrilege, so if you love it and it works for you, then stop reading this bit now and skip to the next section.

Here we go. For me gratitude always seems predicated by *ought* and *should,* as in, you *ought* to be grateful for your health/home/good income or you *should* be grateful for the food on the table. There are lots of starving children in Africa – sort of thing.

This word I like

I prefer *appreciate*. It carries no remonstrance or guilt-trip for me. It means more or less the same thing as gratitude, but with slightly different connotations. It is more about valuing, noticing, being conscious of or placing a high estimate on. I like that. It's good to appreciate things and people in your life.

My favorite word

The other day I stumbled across another word that expresses similar feelings, but in a way I like even better. It made me tingle with recognition. It's a well-known word, but not used all that often in everyday conversation.

This word was in a book called *Getting Stoned With Savages: A Trip Through the Islands of Fiji and Vanuatu,* by J Maarten Troost. How's that for a title? A little un-PC I guess, but still, I'm so jealous.

It was recommended to me by my equally rebellious and curmudgeon-in-crime niece, Sally, so I couldn't resist downloading it.

Here's the quote. See if you can spot the word before I tell you what it is.

"For what is life, a good life, but the accumulation of small pleasures? In Washington, we lived in a place where everything was available, for a price and yet I couldn't recall the last time I had really savored something – a book, a sunset, a fine meal."

There. There it is. *Savored.* That word just jumped off the page at me, daring me to ignore it.

Savor. That works better for me than gratitude. I want to *savor* life, everything about it, appreciate it, experience it, even the smallest of details.

Savor reminds me of chocolate – you put that truffle on your tongue and know you have to savor every moment of it before it disappears forever. You know it's not a good idea to have another (well, maybe one more) or you will feel sick. But this first bite is just heaven and you want to enjoy it fully. When you savor something you totally appreciate it with all your senses.

I want to approach life like that. When I step out into my garden in the morning I *savor* the soft sunshine (unless I'm in England and then I savor the rain and chilly breeze.) I savor looking at the trees and I savor watching my dogs playing. I know they won't always be with me, like the chocolate, so I savor every tiny moment with them.

The lessons from nearly dying

Eckhart Tolle, the great writer and spiritual teacher, says he enjoys reading about near death experiences because it seems to be the closest any of us will come to proof of what happens when we die. Everything else is just speculation. He notes how, despite the differences in what is experienced or who people meet up with while journeying to the other side – Jesus, parents, Buddha, Yogananda, a spirit group and a plethora of different scenes such as tunnels, beautiful palaces, brightly lit scenes from nature – everyone seems to come back with the attitude that *all is well*.

They also have a new perspective on life and most never again take anything for granted. They *savor* the life they have left. Every second. And are filled with purpose.

Ok, I guess they are grateful to be back in the land of the living, but strangely not completely. Sometimes they resist being sent back, at least initially, because their experience of the afterlife is so incredibly blissful and interesting. And when they return everything is changed, different. They seem able to experience and enjoy life more than before. They've been given a second chance. They can accept whatever is happening. All is well.

Gary Zukav in his wonderful book, *The Seat of the Soul*, refers to this emotion as *reverence* for life. That's another good word that resonates with me. He says,

> *"Reverence is simply the experience of accepting that all Life is, in and of itself, of value. If we perceived life with reverence and understood our evolutionary process, we*

would stand in awe at the experience of physical Life and walk the Earth with a very deep sense of gratitude."

Oh, I know. He uses the G-word there. But it's in reference to reverence. And I like the way he uses it, as acceptance. If I'm accepting life as it is, I'm not complaining or feeling sorry for myself. I'm grateful and appreciative and I don't take anything for granted.

How about this idea: It always seems to be the 'good' things we are grateful for. How about being able to accept and flow with everything that happens to us, things we judge as fortunate or unfortunate? We are truly blessed when we can enjoy everything in life – good and bad – and savor whatever weather greets us each day.

Recently I was grousing to my friend Sharyn about how the word gratitude didn't work for me.

She said, *"Hold on, I heard a phrase the other day on YouTube or a podcast, can't remember where and it makes a perfect mantra*."

"Try this; first thing when you wake up say, *I am the essence of gratitude*; when you step outside, say *I am the essence of gratitude*; when you go to sleep, say *I am the essence of gratitude.* At every moment in the day, when you remember say, *I am the essence of gratitude*. You don't have to say for *what* you are grateful, unless you feel like it, or to *whom*, just that you embody gratitude. See if that works for you."

Well, it does work. It's a powerful mantra. Say it all day, all the time, for everything, every experience, without judgment. It completely reframes the idea of gratitude for me. It takes it away from the objects to be thankful for and expresses an appreciation of simply being alive.

So I guess the word doesn't really matter as long as it takes you to a place that feels empowering and significant. Who cares what the word is if it is life enhancing?

This works.

I want to be able to savor, reverence, walk the Earth with a very deep sense of gratitude and enjoy every moment, taking the good with the bad. Just as if I had been given a new lease on life – a second chance. That seems to me to be what living my purpose and following the trail of my spirit is all about.

Now: Your mission, should you choose to accept it...

...is to write your mission statement. It doesn't have to be perfect. Just answer the questions that follow and start writing. It should feel good to write it and then to read it. Your mission statement is a statement about your values, attitudes and goals. It's a testament as to how you want to live your life. What you choose to do for your work or activity needs to align with this statement in order for you to begin to live authentically.

And a powerful coaching question to get you started:

If you were going to write a book about your life, what would be the theme?

Here are the prompts for formulating your mission statement:

My life purpose, right here, right now, is to...

I do this by (or through)...

Every day I want to...

My personal goal is to...

Formulate your mission statement with infinitives, action verbs, e.g. to inspire, to connect, to serve, to encourage, to motivate.

Finish these sentences to write your statement.
My own personal statement is this:

> *My life purpose right now is to help people get their lives to work.*
>
> *I do this through coaching, writing, workshops.*
>
> *Every day I strive to connect, to serve, to inspire, to motivate and encourage the people I come in contact with.*
>
> *My personal goal is to grow spiritually, through study, practice and rigorous self-development.*

Remember, life purpose is also about **who you want to be**. So in addition I want to be someone who:

> *Encourages those who feel dispirited.*
>
> *Supports those who feel unsupported.*
>
> *Listens to those who don't feel heard.*
>
> *Inspires and motivates those who are trying their best.*
>
> *Coaches those who need someone to tell them the truth.*

Hey, we're nearly there. Let's pull this all together and set out on the trail of your spirit. It's time to go.

Coaching question:

What job does your life resumé prepare you for? It is a unique position and you are the only one qualified for it!

Chapter 11

Following the Trail of Your Spirit

"To every thing there is a season,
and a time to every purpose under the heaven:
A time to be born, a time to die;
a time to plant,
and a time to pluck up that which is planted."
– Ecclesiastes 3:1-2

At different times in your life, your spirit trail will lead you in different directions.

Consider my friend Denise, who found her niche in her 60s.

For years Denise had struggled with money and financial security seemed to elude her. She had the archetype *Hedonist* and loved the good things in life – fine wine, nice restaurants, designer clothes, shoes, bags, makeup, hair, nails, spas for relaxation and retreat from all the stress of shopping and spending. Nice vacations. But she was always in debt.

Eventually, her financial problems came to a head and she couldn't meet her rent deadline. This embarrassing crisis was the final straw and the fear and sleepless nights convinced her to change her whole approach to the way she was living.

Instead of always striving after more money to pay for all her stuff, she decided her ticket to freedom lay in needing less stuff and embracing a lower maintenance way of living. When she worked out how much her purchases cost her and how little joy they had brought her, she decided something had to go. That something was her lifestyle.

She started watching YouTube videos on minimalist living. She stopped going out for expensive meals and started cooking at home and shopping in the local market. She was astounded how much she could buy for so little. She started frequenting flea markets and second hand stores and picked up some gorgeous clothes for a pittance. She did her own grooming and even started helping her friends to save on their makeup and hair costs. Many of her friends commented on how much better she was looking. This made her chuckle.

She moved to a smaller and less expensive apartment, which was cheaper to heat and run. She loved it. It was cozy.

After a few months of this new regime she noticed she had money in her bank account at the end of the month, instead of an overdraft. She found this new way of living satisfying and interestingly, so much fun that she couldn't remember ever living differently. She felt self-confident and self-sufficient for the first time in her life and became a sort of authority on living frugally, helping others turn on to a minimalist lifestyle. But most importantly to her, it gave her a sense of control over her life and the feeling that she didn't have to be a victim to her habits.

Denise had found her niche. Was this her *life* purpose, I hear you ask? Yes, for this time in her life. A life purpose doesn't have to be some magnificent obsession or profession. *It can be whatever brings meaning and value and interest to your day-to-day life. Right now.*

Denise's thrifty lifestyle made her more aware of waste and how we are hurting the environment with our throwaway habits. It became a sort of spiritual quest for her and brought her in touch with being human and able to survive on this planet. It had meaning for her.

But it's important to note: she probably could not have embraced it with such gusto at any other time in her life. She had to experience the consequences of being indulgent and careless with her resources, to descend to the point where she knew she had to change. This is why there is no reason to regret or bemoan the shortcomings of the past: they are the catalyst for what you can become now. You needed all those mistakes and missed opportunities and losses in order to be where you are now.

Only then can you *leap like a jaguar into what you are becoming.*

The Four Directions

A few years ago, out of curiosity I took a course in Shamanism 101. I wanted to learn more about who shamans were and what they got up to and discover if there was anything in it relevant to my life. (Here was my *Seeker*, in active mode. Something new to learn? Where do I sign up?)

As it turned out, I loved the course and have used a number of the techniques and tenets in my work and daily life ever since. But one teaching really stood out for me and I refer to it time and again. It is pertinent to our discussion here.

You may have heard of it before.

It's referred to as *the Four Directions* and can be found in Native American teachings, Shamanism, Paganism, Druidism and other indigenous practices. Some call it the Medicine Wheel. All ancient civilizations, including the Aztecs and the Egyptians, regard the Four Directions as sacred.

It uses the four cardinal points – North, East, South, West – as symbolic of the four elements (earth, air, fire, water), the seasons (winter, spring, summer, fall), the times of the day (midnight, sunrise, noon and sunset). Each direction has a unique vibration, a spirit animal, an attribute, meaning and wisdom.

The spirit of each direction can be invoked and called upon for help in decision making, in surviving life transitions and in finding your path when you are lost in the forest. It operates as a kind of life compass to help you orient yourself when times are tough.

Here is a description of each direction:

Direction North

Earth element, midnight, winter, spirit animal buffalo, wisdom of letting go, letting things die so that the spring can come with new growth. Allowing the ground to lie fallow.

Meaning: there are times in life that we need the North energies to accept the transition of death. What do you need to let go in your life? What needs to die so there is room for the new? This may be a time to grieve.

The energies of the spirit animal buffalo teach us to be patient and survive the harsh cold of the Northern Winter. A new day always dawns.

Attributes: patience, transition, faith in the coming of the dawn.

Direction East

Air element, sunrise, spring, spirit animal eagle. New beginnings, fresh starts, initiating new projects.

Meaning: you can always start anew in life. The dawn always comes if you have patience and can survive the fears of the night.

The energies of eagle assist us in finding the guiding vision of our lives.

Attributes: hope, innocence, renewal, optimism, vision, setting goals, seeing the big picture, making plans.

Direction South
Fire element, noon, summer, spirit animal grey wolf. Wisdom of taking inspired action, passion, movement.

Meaning: there is a time to act as well as a time to rest and reflect. If we don't act, nothing will happen in our lives. At some point we must stop planning and dreaming and leap into the fray.

The energies of wolf assist us to act with wisdom and when we do, to be fierce.

Attributes: passion, engagement, action.

Direction West
Water element, sunset, autumn, spirit animal jaguar. Time for transformation, reflection, taking stock and altering course if necessary. This is the time to gather in, reap the harvest and reflect.

Meaning: at times we need to sit back and reflect, gather our resources and enjoy the fruits of our labors. Time to stop frantic activity and focus on what is important.

The energies of jaguar assist us to be still, observe and choose carefully when to leap.

Attributes: adaptability, change, gaining perspective, developing wisdom.

Stages of life

Each direction also corresponds to stages in our lives. We can see that the East/Spring represents youth, South/Summer our young adult years, West/Autumn middle age and North/Winter our elder years.

What direction are you in now? Each stage of life can have a different purpose and needs a different perspective and energy. Your purpose will most certainly change as you evolve, grow. Your purpose at retirement may be very different from your purpose in your 20s.

Have you avoided putting your toe in one of the directions? If so how can you bring it into your life? If we want to live fully, on purpose and with balance and equilibrium we need to circle around all four directions and make sure each area is healthy.

Each epoch in your life can have its own purpose.

Each year can have a new purpose.

Each day can have a new purpose.

Treat each day as a lifetime. What do I want my life to be about today?

And remember that every thing you do can have value.

The search for *life purpose* is really and truly a search to find the real you and you can find it through the right activities.

Are you kind?

Look after animals?

Care for plants?

Live minimally?

Recycle?

Keep in touch with people?

You are enough!

Are you someone people can turn to?

You are enough!

Do you listen to people?

You are enough!

Everything that has happened in your life and every stage of your life is useful – the good and the bad. You learn, develop values, life skills, wisdom and perspective from everything that you have experienced. Your past is a gold mine you are sitting on, or ignoring and it's just waiting to be exploited. Nothing needs to be wasted. The only waste is despair, or guilt, or regret.

Following the trail of your Spirit

Now you're on the trail. The journey is just beginning. Stay alert and awake. And remember to keep watching, watching, always watching.

"You follow by intuition and observation.
The trail will be clear of obstacles.
When off the trail, many obstacles will be found.
When you meet resistance, you are off the trail.
Look for happenings, look for signs.
You must feel your way along, carefully watching,
watching, always watching." – Hopi Shaman

When you are off the trail obstacles appear. Get back on the trail.

Sometimes the trail can disappear for days, weeks, months, or years. Big life transitions can leave you bewildered, lost in the forest. You need to stop, cocoon, wait, observe. The trail will show itself to you in its own time. Leap back on the trail. It's waiting for you.

When you're following your trail you're neither stuck nor lost.

You feel like you're getting somewhere.

You feel like you're heading in the right direction

You feel like you're on track.

And when you are on the trail, living your purpose, you feel aligned, congruent, excited. Purpose unfolds, moves, disappears for while and then reappears in a new guise. It's an ever-evolving journey.

"Wake up! It is never too late to reconstruct your life. Analyze what you are and what your soul-appointed tasks are, so that you can make yourself what you should be."
– Yogananda

Wake up! and find your true identity.

Wake up! and find authenticity.

Wake up! and find your voice.

Wake up! and find the rapture of being alive.

Wake up! to a life well spent.

Wayne Dyer, self-help author and motivational speaker, used to say,

"Don't die with your music in you."

What is your music? Go find it. Leap on the trail and follow the music.

Epilogue

A few weeks after I sent this book to my editor I was watching a video on YouTube of an English Vedanta teacher named Rupert Spira. It was a question and answer session and the questioner asked Rupert specifically, *"What is the goal of life?"*

He answered without hesitation and with some firmness, *"The goal of life is happiness."*

That was it. Happiness. Period.

I wondered why I had written this book. The answer to *what should I do with my life* is so simple. I could have saved us all a lot of trouble and I fear I have only complicated the issue.

I can only hope that some of the content may help you find happiness – happy work, happy lifestyle, happy retirement, happy mind.

If this book points you even a little in that direction I will be happy, so we both win.

Margaret Nash
San Miguel de Allende, Mexico
March 2019

Did you like what you just read?

If so I would LOVE and APPRECIATE a nice review. Reviews help indie authors more than you can possibly imagine.

I will even buy you lunch if you're ever in San Miguel de Allende, Mexico.

That's a promise—tacos on me.

Just go to the page on amazon.com for ***Follow the Trail of Your Spirit*** and click on reviews – or use this link:

getbook.at/follow-trail

Please download my FREE e-book

The Rebellious Entrepreneur

5 crucial steps to help you establish yourself profess-ionally and make a success of your business or practice.

Find your voice, your identity, and position yourself in the marketplace.

Get it now!

www.margaretnashcoach.com/5-steps

Would you like to work online with Margaret Nash?

Professional, affordable, first class Life–Coaching that will guarantee results in your life and work. Watch your productivity soar with as you create good work habits, motivational goals, and strategies for manifesting the life you want.

Find out more about her online ***Life-Coaching*** at

www.margaretnashcoach.com/life-coaching

We use Facebook Messenger or Zoom. No video.

Pay for each session via PayPal—simple, easy, quick.

Check it out

www.margaretnashcoach.com/life-coaching

What's your next big step in life? Try *Life-Coaching* and make it happen!

About Margaret Nash

Margaret Nash lives and works as a writer, life coach, seminar leader, wife, dog owner, and friend who will lunch at the drop of a hat, in San Miguel de Allende in the Central Highlands of Mexico.

She grew up in Alabama, in the 1960s, and after college visited England and stayed for three decades.

Margaret's blog, and her books, *Rebellious Aging, Drop the Drama! How to Get Along With Everybody, All the Time, The Retirement Rebel, Artful Assertiveness Skills for Women,* and *Follow the Trail of Your Spirit*, deal with the themes of aging well, surviving transitions, and finding your niche in life in your 50s, 60s, and beyond.

Her demographic is the *rebel/hippie at heart/fiercely independent free spirit* facing major life changes and determined to age in the coolest way possible.

Margaret is a Master Practitioner & Trainer/Coach in NLP, Hypnosis and Time-line Therapy. She has been in practice for 17 years.

She is a certified aging brat/skeptic/seeker/searcher— and definitely a hippie at heart.

www.margaretnashcoach.com

Aging can be fun! You just need to awaken your Rebel and survive those transitions.

This book is a motivational, self-help guide for you if you are a hippie at heart— in other words unconventional, fiercely independent and a bit of a rebel—determined to find your niche in life and enjoy yourself as you grow older.

It is a book about transitions; the transitions of life that sometimes hit you hard, like retirement, kids leaving home, divorce, relocation … or waking up one morning and realizing you are no longer a spring chicken.

So hop into your hippie van and take a Hero's Journey down into your subconscious mind to find your true self, your authentic voice, and practical and effective ways to survive all the changes piling up on you.

The methods and processes included here can't be found in the doctor's office or on a psychoanalyst's couch. They are unorthodox and will appeal to the hippie in you. But don't be mislead—this book contains effective life-coaching tips and techniques for personal inner transformation.

Download your kindle copy today:

getbook.at/rebellious-aging

You may also enjoy *Drop the Drama! How to Get Along With Everybody, All the Time* also by Margaret Nash, available in kindle and paperback on Amazon.

Do You Want a Drama Free Life? Then Drop the Drama!

Are you tired of squabbling, trying to make amends with people you have offended, or clearing up misunderstandings? Sick of dealing with your own hurt feelings?

Look no further. Read this book!

Adopt these skills and rock all relationships!

It's possible to turn over a new leaf right now. You absolutely can learn how to *get along with everybody, all the time*, no matter who you are, how cantankerous, and despite any past relationship disasters.

But you are going to have to learn to play nice, even when you don't feel like it. You can do this.

So I invite you to absorb this book and put your nose to the grindstone practicing the **six social skills** outlined—until they become second nature. You will be glad you did.

In this easy to read self-help guide:

- Be introduced to the ***Most Useful Relationship Technique Ever in the History of the Universe*** (no hyperbole!).
- Find out how to avoid being the ***least popular type of person***.

- Discover your **personality style** and how you can use it to get along with everybody.
- Learn the ***secret sauce*** to fabulous relationships.

These skills are culled from the cutting-edge life enhancing techniques of **Neuro-linguistic Programming**, along with a plethora of tried and true skills from Don Miguel Ruiz, to Dale Carnegie, to Eckhart Tolle.

Once you 'get' them everything will become easier and you will create **stress-free, ruffled-feather-free relationships** with everyone in your life. That's a promise!

If you have recently retired, or are planning for retirement you may like my book, ***The Retirement Rebel: How to get your life to work when you don't have to*** available in Kindle and paperback on Amazon.

Want to Make Your Retirement Rock?

Thinking of retiring? Ready to relocate to sunnier climes, free from responsibilities, schedules, and alarm clocks? And absolutely determined this will be the best time of your life?

Wait! **Read this first**! *U.S. News & World Report* tells us that the typical retiree today spends four hours a day watching television. You don't want that!

And many retirees report feeling stuck, blue, disappointed and wondering why the heck they are so bored relaxing in the Costa Rica sun sipping Margaritas. Hello?

The truth is, retirement is an ***enormous life transition*** that can trip you up if you're not vigilant. Or it can be the best, most fabulous time of your life!

It's like a huge tidal wave of change sweeping over you.

Read this book if you want to be prepared!

Welcome to The Retirement Rebel, an entertaining, practical, and sometimes surprising self-help guide for those who are ready to retire and committed to making it work from the get-go.

This is not a book about pensions, savings, insurance, or health plans. *Snooze.*

Instead, it will show you how to avoid ***4 major retirement pitfalls*** and ensure you find your feet, hit the ground running, and best of all, do it your way. Like a rebel.

- Discover the #1 reason you can get stuck and how to avoid it
- Realize exactly why you get the blues and what you can do about it
- Uncover what it is you really miss about work… and it may surprise you.

This book is your insurance policy against those pitfalls. Read it and you're covered. Comprehensive policy. Full indemnity against the blues and full warranty for a great retirement.

Download your kindle copy today:

getbook.at/retirement-rebel

Ladies, if you suffer from not being heard or taken seriously, ***Artful Assertiveness Skills for Women,* By Margaret Nash** may be the book for you!

Attention Ladies of all ages, shapes, sizes, and personalities! Would you like to learn how to stand up for yourself, gain respect, and handle *every* situation with calm assurance and authority? Yes?

Then you need to read this book! It's time for **Assertiveness Boot Camp** and this book is your self-help Boot Camp Guide.

So pull on your fatigues, lace up your boots, and let's get to work!

Welcome to *Artful Assertiveness Skills for Women.*

Here you will learn the basic rules of assertiveness:

- Learn how to say no, artfully and effectively without anyone getting upset.
- Define and protect your boundaries without anyone noticing.
- Project a calm, confident energy that will make the Dog Whisperer jealous.
- Shut down bullies and passive-aggressive, catty types with style and wit.
- Learn the body language that will ensure you are listened to and taken seriously. Avoid these seven common mistakes.
- Practice the best way to complain about bad service.

- Discover how to keep yourself safe both physically and emotionally.

But it takes some work! You'll going to learn some awesome and artful responses that will just trip off your tongue the next time you are upset, ignored, or challenged.

You will also pick up some very useful body language tips that may save your bacon one day and learn the secret of how to exude an energy that makes people sit up, listen and treat you with respect.

This self-help guide is fun, easy to read and will keep you entertained with real life stories to illustrate how assertiveness works, or doesn't work.

You'll get Boot Camp homework—phrases and sentences to practice—after every chapter. You can literally just copy down useful responses and use them verbatim.

It's different from other assertiveness training—it really emphasizes the artful bit— which means you always come across as natural, friendly and relaxed while still getting the respect you deserve.

This is the 4th book in the *Hippie at Heart Self-help Series* by Margaret Nash, Life-Coach, Business Trainer, NLP Master Practitioner, self-help writer, aging brat, hippie at heart…as she shares her years of experience with clients, family, friends, dogs and cats, honing her assertiveness skills. (OK, it didn't work with the cats.)

What people are saying about Artful Assertiveness Skills for Women:

"This book has so much valuable advice on modern life for the modern woman. You'll learn how to handle difficult people and stressful situations --without stress! Margaret Nash offers a

refreshing perspective on women's issues in the workplace and in day-to-day interactions." SP Ericson

"This is a timely book. The rise of the ***MeToo*** *movement spawns stories indicating far too many women lack skills in assertiveness. Standing up in situations where power is the undercurrent is hard. This is an important book. Nash's chapter on creating boundaries and another on 'combat training' made this an especially good read. Buy this for you.... and your daughters."* Barbara Pagano

"I teach assertiveness skills in my business and LOVE this book! Margaret provides clear stories and solutions so that reader's assertiveness muscles will get bigger and bigger as they flex their healthy, compassionate, courageous power." Trina

"This book delivers ~ chapter after chapter after chapter ~ and percolates along with such an upbeat and companionable delivery that the reader cannot help but gain an infusion of the Artful Assertiveness Skills author Margaret Nash promises!"

"While she employs such yang training metaphors as "Boot Camp" and "Test Pilots," she does so in a manner that serves the yin value of relationship: attaining these aptitudes not for "power-over" ends, but in order to cultivate win-win accord. As this book is written with women in mind, this is most satisfactory in terms of Jungian Psychology, which teaches that a woman's animus, or masculine dimension, is there to serve her womanly nature." Mary Trainor-Brigham

"Up 'til now I have been the kind of woman who usually said 'yes' when I really meant 'no'! Reading Margaret Nash's book has encouraged me to be more authentic with my real feelings with a new courage to speak my truth without being abrasive.

Having been a 'nice girl' all of my life, I was a natural people pleaser and generally said what people wanted to hear.

I'm very encouraged after reading and practicing 'Artful Assertiveness Skills for Women' and I'm enjoying this newfound freedom... my communication skills have become more forthright. I have used many of the suggestions in this book ... especially the one of asking questions like, 'now why would you say that?' or 'What do you mean by that comment?' A question seems to stop an aggressive person in their tracks and the dynamic quickly changes. So far, I've not offended any of my friends and have a much better relationship with my employee who thought she was boss! I highly recommend." Sabrina

"This book lays out a concise, easy plan or boot camp for improving daily interactions with every person you encounter. With lists of exact actions & dialogues to facilitate desired outcomes, I wasn't surprised the author has spent much of her career as a life coach. It doesn't read like a self-help book, but more as an action plan to guide us toward results. Easy & interesting read. Wish I had access to this at age 20 instead of 50!" Krista Yarnell

"Bought at book at the local library for my 25 year old daughter and she loved it! Never too early or late to start learning this stuff!" Joseph Toone

Made in the USA
Las Vegas, NV
29 March 2023